PENGUIN

THE FIRE OF LOVE

ADVISORY EDITOR: BETTY RADICE

RICHARD ROLLE was born about the year 1300 at Thornton-le-dale in Yorkshire. He studied at Oxford until he was nineteen and left without a degree. Back in Yorkshire he ran away from home after making a rough and ready hermit's habit out of his father's rain-hood and two of his sister's frocks. The next day he found a patron in the Constable of Pickering Castle, John de Dalton, who gave him food and anchorage. But his mystical extremes aroused the hostility of the local clergy and monks, whom he roundly rebukes in his *Judica me, Deus* and *Melos Amoris*. He seems never to have been ordained or licensed as a hermit, but his influence was wide and his writing prolific. A certain testy independence steered him through many a change of friend and protector. But as he matured so he mellowed, and before his death on Michaelmas Day 1349 he had become the spiritual director of all Cistercian nuns at Hampole, near Doncaster. He was the author of a rich and varied body of writing in the vernacular and his *Fire of Love*, composed in 1343, is the best known of his works. Soon a cult of 'St Richard Hermit' had grown up, and some thirty years after his death a succession of miracles were reported at his tomb. Although never officially recognized as a saint he continued to be so revered until the Reformation.

CLIFTON WOLTERS was born in London and trained for the priesthood at Durham University and the London College of Divinity. He was Vicar of Wimbledon Park, Rector of Sanderstead, and later Provost of Newcastle. Upon retirement he became Provost Emeritus and Chaplain to the Society of St Margaret. He also translated *The Cloud of Unknowing* and Julian of Norwich's *Revelations of Divine Love* for Penguin Classics. He died in 1991.

The
FIRE
of
LOVE

RICHARD ROLLE

Translated into modern English
with an introduction by
CLIFTON WOLTERS

Penguin Books

PENGUIN BOOKS

Published by the Penguin Group
Penguin Books Ltd, 27 Wrights Lane, London W8 5TZ, England
Penguin Books USA Inc., 375 Hudson Street, New York, New York 10014, USA
Penguin Books Australia Ltd, Ringwood, Victoria, Australia
Penguin Books Canada Ltd, 10 Alcorn Avenue, Toronto, Ontario, Canada M4V 3B2
Penguin Books (NZ) Ltd, 182–190 Wairau Road, Auckland 10, New Zealand

Penguin Books Ltd, Registered Offices: Harmondsworth, Middlesex, England

This translation first published 1972
5 7 9 10 8 6

Printed in England by Clays Ltd, St Ives plc
Set in Linotype Georgian

CONTENTS

CONTENTS

INTRODUCTION

F E w books of medieval devotion can have got off to a more intriguing start than *The Fire of Love*. One can still sense the surprise passing into delight that seized Richard Rolle as he ran his hand over his chest to see if he were actually on fire. Yet this was no calculated trick designed to trap a reluctant reader to go on with what would do him good even if it bored him in the process, but an expression of what was to Richard a fact. The whole book is a defence of the phenomenon, supplying the reasons for an experience, but not perhaps a real explanation of his temperature.

For Rolle had no need of literary devices to draw attention to his books. He was a prolific writer in both Latin and English, and had a wide circle of readers. He was a pioneer of writing in the vernacular, and it is with some degree of accuracy that he has been called 'the true father of English literature'.[1] Such was his reputation that apart from those works known to be genuine (they cover commentaries, treatises, scriptural translations, and smaller pieces) many other manuscripts mostly anonymous were ascribed to him by medieval enthusiasts.

The Fire of Love is an untidy sort of book, repetitive, enthusiastic, dogmatic, and heart-warming. Whatever Rolle wrote he wrote with verve and energy. He had a feel for words, and he loved using them. His story is that he has had, and is still having, profound mystical experiences, and as his prologue says he 'would stir up by these means every man to love God'; so he writes them down, not once or twice but again and again. This makes *The Fire* difficult to analyse, for the book goes on in great circular sweeps, saying much the same thing each time, and yet adding a

1. C. Horstmann, *Yorkshire Writers: Richard Rolle and his followers*, volume 2, p. xxv.

little here, a little there, catching it all up into the next swinging movement.

Yet for all his repetitiousness Rolle is rarely tedious. There are at least four reasons for this:
(i) His skill in the choice of language and the variety with which he sets it out. (ii) His knack of bringing in something new the next time round. (iii) The vastness of the theme he is patently trying to get over. (iv) The artlessness with which he writes. For all his mastery of words one gets the impression that he is writing as his heart dictates and not his head. He is one of the great medieval poets, and not all poets can write prose plain and unadorned. And when he is writing of the mysteries of the spirit, deeply felt and known, it is impossible for him to be flat, whether he is using Latin as here, or, as so often, English. In some ways his style can be compared to that of a great symphony in which the melody is introduced, and reintroduced in a variety of ways as each movement develops and fresh themes are taken up.

The Fire of Love is, as has just been implied, an English translation of Rolle's most famous work, *Incendium Amoris*. Its widespread popularity is shown in the abundance of surviving manuscripts, for there are over forty copies of the *Incendium* still in existence, none later than the early fifteenth century.[2] It survives in two versions, one three-fifths the length of the other. The shorter is demonstrably an abridgement of the longer, and has cut out all the autobiographical and specifically theological sections. In some instances the short manuscripts have been combined with Rolle's commentary on the Canticles (or Song of Songs) in a confusing series of permutations. The short version is thought to have been prepared by a religious, and, as it stands, gives a concise summary of the hermit's teaching on the contemplative life. This present translation is based on the longer text.

---

2. The British Museum has five, Cambridge six, Oxford nine, and the rest of the country seven. There are a further fourteen copies in Continental countries.

But if a broad analysis of *The Fire* is wanted, few would quarrel with Dr Margaret Deanesly when she thus describes it:

It is rather a series of discourses on subjects connected with the life of a solitary than a complete didactic scheme. In the prologue, Rolle states his own desire to prove to others the joy of the life he has chosen; the next eleven chapters are devoted to considerations preliminary to the undertaking of such a life; then come two chapters where he passes from advice to autobiography. The remaining chapters are mainly a series of discourses strung together with no particular plan, on the various difficulties of the contemplative life.[3]

THE WRITER

More is known about Richard Rolle than about any other English mystic of the fourteenth century. Even so it is little enough. But whereas in the case of Mother Julian and Walter Hilton we depend on scattered contemporary references, and the occasional autobiographical details they give, for Rolle there are not only these sources, but also the *Legenda*[1] compiled by the nuns of Hampole against the day of his canonization, a labour of love that somehow got lost. More than most Rolle wrote himself into his works and they supply further information. Yet with it all it still does not amount to very much, even though for his period it is generous, and more than might be expected.

Many manuscripts say that he died on Michaelmas Day, 1349, and it is conjectured that he was a victim of the appalling plague then decimating Europe, the Black Death. But when he was born can only be guesswork. The year 1300 or thereabouts is the one most favoured. In his *Melos*

3. *Incendium Amoris*, p. 41.
1. After his death, and perhaps before, Rolle was regarded as a saint, and in preparation for his canonization an office was drawn up. The *Legenda* were the edifying lessons, nine in number, to be read at Mattins on his feast day.

Amoris he describes himself as a young man. In this book there is, some scholars suggest, a reference to the infidelities of Queen Isabella with Roger Mortimer. This royal scandal was more than a talking point of 1325–6. It involved national disaster, the abdication of Edward II, and his murder. If there is a reference here to current affairs then the turn of the century or a few years earlier might be the natal period. There is no reliable alternative.

Whatever may be thought about the date of his birth there is a strong likelihood that we know where it took place. The 'village of Thornton near Pickering in the diocese of York', says the *Legenda*, and though Yorkshire has sixteen villages so named, that of Thornton-le-dale has always claimed the honour. From the same source it is learned that his father's name was William. Presumably he was not a wealthy man, for Richard was sponsored at Oxford by Thomas Neville, Archdeacon of Durham. There he stayed till he was nineteen, 'making great progress in study'. The course at Oxford in his day lasted seven years for a Master's degree, and the inference is that he came down without one, having removed himself lest he should get his values mixed and his priorities wrong. Clearly at university Rolle, like many another undergraduate, faced, perhaps for the first time, the fundamental 'why' of existence, and the fact of sin, and took action in reply.

Back in Yorkshire, he literally ran away from home to become a hermit. The strange story of his fashioning a rough-and-ready hermit's habit out of his father's rain-hood and two of his sister's frocks (more difficult today!) has often been told. It is worth hearing again, and here it is in the pious language of the hagiographer, who possibly tolerated this earnest, light-fingered charade because of its outcome:

After he had returned from Oxford to his father's house, he said one day to his sister, who loved him with tender affection: 'My beloved sister, thou hast two tunics which I greatly covet, one white and the other grey. Therefore I ask thee if thou will kindly give them to me, and bring them tomorrow to the wood near by, together with my father's rain-hood.' She agreed willingly, and the next day according to her promise, carried them to the said wood, being quite ignorant of what was in her brother's mind. And when he had received them he straightway cut off the sleeves from the grey tunic and the buttons from the white, and as best he could he fitted the sleeves to the white tunic, so that they might in some manner be suited to his purpose. Then he took off his own clothes with which he was clad and put on his sister's tunic next his skin, but the grey, with the sleeves cut out, he put over it, and put his arms through the holes which had been cut; and he covered his head with the rain-hood aforesaid, so that in some measure, as far as then was in his power, he might present a certain likeness to a hermit. But when his sister saw this she was astounded and cried: 'My brother is mad! My brother is mad!' Whereupon he drove her from him with threats, and fled himself at once without delay, lest he should be seized upon by his friends and acquaintances.[2]

There was more melodrama to follow. He fled to a nearby church to pray. It could have been Dalton, a score of miles away over the moors; it might have been Pickering – both villages were associated with him – and near Thornton. It was the eve of the Assumption. Unwittingly (can one be quite sure of this?) he knelt in the place customarily occupied by the lady of the manor, and either because he was excited or, more likely, rapt in prayer, did not budge when she came in with her sons for Vespers. Her servants were for moving him, but she would not have his prayer disturbed, and he was left in possession. After Vespers the young men recognized him as a fellow Oxonian.

It is not known where he spent the night. Had it been in vigil the *Legenda* would have been delighted. But they are silent. Probably it was with the parish priest, for in the morning Rolle is found in church again, surpliced, and singing Mattins. And at the Mass, after the Gospel, with the celebrant's blessing, he mounts the pulpit and preaches a sermon of such sincerity and beauty that 'the multitude

2. *Legenda*. Lesson 1; translated by Miss F. M. M. Comper in her *Life of Richard Rolle*, p. 302.

could not refrain from tears', saying 'they had never before heard a sermon of such virtue and power'.

After Mass, John de Dalton, squire of the village of the same name and Constable of Pickering Castle, took him home to a meal, and to the inevitable slump of reaction. Dalton is said to have been a self-made and ruthless character, but he must also have been a man of considerable perspicacity, for he got the whole story out of Richard, and unlike his friend William, the boy's father, recognized the genuineness of his vocation to the solitary life. In this conviction he kitted him out with clothes more suitable for a hermit, and most generously provided him with the shelter and food he needed to prove the experiment.

With Richard launched the *Legenda* give no more examples of dramatic incident. They relate the experience set out in the prologue to *The Fire*, and go on to describe a curious incident when he was visited by

the lady of the house, and many other persons with her, and they found him writing very quickly. And they besought him to leave off writing and speak a word of edification to them, which he immediately did, exhorting them most eloquently to virtue, and to renounce worldly vanities and stablish the love of God in their hearts. Yet in no way on account of this did he cease writing for two hours without interruption, but continued to write as quickly as before. . . . The occupations were discrepant one from another, and the spoken words differed utterly in meaning from those which he wrote.

This discourteous way of treating female guests suggests that there still lingered a certain uncouthness about Rollé (who might have had the gift of automatic writing), but the pious author saw in it the action of the Holy Spirit. On another occasion Rolle was troubled by a beautiful woman who turned out to be the devil, for she vanished as he signed himself with the Cross, and recollected the Precious Blood. An account of an exorcism is followed by a mention of various moves of abode, beneficial to his new neighbours, but giving scope to the malevolence of certain detractors. A couple of miracles affecting a recluse of Richmondshire,

Margaret Kirkby, are followed by an excerpt from *The Fire* (chapter 15) describing the spiritual gifts of heat, sweetness, and melody.

The *Legenda* seem to play down the troubles Rolle describes in the autobiographical parts of his writings. Perhaps he felt them at the time more keenly than later reflection saw them to be: in any case he himself seems to have contributed to their provocation, for his earlier writings reveal him as a fiery young man, seeing things as black or white, and possessing a certain power of invective. At that time he found it difficult to offer the other cheek; he tended to hit back. In the *Judica Me* and the *Melos Amoris*, for example, both products of his youth, he expresses himself freely on the local clergy and monks and on his detractors generally – rarely to their advantage. This they did not find endearing, and understandably he met with considerable opposition and criticism. It is likely that his attacks were justified, but the tender years of the self-appointed scourge (who in any case stood outside the system) did not help his case.

It seems that his hermit life began irregularly, for there is no record of his having been licensed or blessed by a bishop either at the beginning or at any time after. We may assume that this omission was ultimately rectified, for the last years seem to have been passed in peace and approval.

His first patron, John de Dalton, was also not without his own worries. He was caught up in the political turmoils and intrigues of those unsettled days, and though he retained his head when Lancaster's rebellion failed he lost his post as Constable of Pickering. His strong personality and Rolle's could clash head on, and it might be reasonable from chapter 15 of *The Fire* to infer that they did.

But apart from these highlights Rolle's life seems to have been peaceful and uneventful, though at times it was very rough. Such is the overall impression given by his writings. Grace and nature softened the prickles and modified the earlier traits, and the later mystic was a much more mellow and balanced person, as the reading of the works of his maturity (for example *The Fire*) will demonstrate. But at every stage, even at his most callow, he was capable of great tenderness and devotion as well as of vigour and reforming zeal.

Towards the end of his life he moved his cell to Hampole, close to Doncaster. Here he directed with much love and patience an anchoress, Margaret Kirkby, who was enclosed at Ainderby,[3] a near-by village, and the sisters of the small Cistercian nunnery at Hampole itself. No trace remains today either of the two cells or of the convent. After his death these same nuns compiled an office in the hope of his canonization, supporting their case with the account of many miracles which were attributed to his intercession or took place at his tomb. But the place of this tomb too has vanished from human memory. There is no record that their plea for the official recognition of his sanctity ever reached Rome. The times were too unsettled. But there is some evidence that until the Reformation a cult of 'St Richard Hermit' existed, and for two hundred years he was widely revered, and his writings were treasured by religious and layfolk alike.

THE HERMIT

Mother Julian was an anchoress, Richard Rolle a hermit. In popular estimation they were doing much the same thing. Yet the difference in fact between the two lives was considerable. All they had in common was that they were *solitaries.*

3. So the *Legenda*. The researches of Miss R. M. Clay and Miss H. E. Allen suggest that the Hampole nuns have telescoped events. It seems that Margaret Kirkby was a nun of Hampole originally, and was enclosed at East Layton in 1348, the year before Rolle died. She was transferred to Ainderby in 1356–7, and later moved back to Hampole round about the 1380s, the time when miracles at Rolle's tomb began to happen. If the evidence of various wills refers to her, she died between 1401 and 1405. The whole matter is discussed with great detail and diligence (and some conjecture) by Miss Allen in her monumental *Writings ascribed to Richard Rolle*, pp. 502–11.

The solitary life or *Eremitism* (to give it its real name) is not a form of living reserved for the unsociable few; most people experience a genuine need to 'get away from it all' from time to time, and that for various reasons. It may be the self-centredness of a Rousseau who wanted solitude 'pour être pleinement moi et à moi', but it may be that of a David who wanted to 'be still and know' the mystery of God. It is not difficult to see how this natural desire can in some cases develop into an attitude that affects the whole life. There can be irreligious hermits as well as religious.

Most of the great religions have made room for the eremitical life. In Christianity the basic impetus surfaced in the fourth century, when the hostile pressure of the government began to ease, and so most forms of hermit living look back to St Antony,[1] the first hermit to acquire wide fame, or past him to a more shadowy St Paul of Thebes.[2] These two heroic solitaries have fathered a rich brood of successors so varied in nature as to defy classification and almost to deny relationship. Yet classification there must be, and the most commonly accepted one is that of Nicolas Boerius,[3] who in his *De Statu et Vita Eremitarum* divided them up under four headings: (i) members of religious communities which bore the title 'hermit', (ii) members of small groups of hermits, living outside the religious state, but whose existence and organization were recognized by episcopal authority; (iii) hermits living in solitude, and licensed as such in the diocese, who often enough undertook some small service in the neighbourhood; (iv) hermits independent of all ecclesiastical recognition and relying upon themselves for everything. This analysis, for all its inadequacy, serves the canonist who can use it to assess whether any particular form of hermit is to be regarded as a member of the religious state or not.

One would like to linger with Boerius' second definition for it has some surprising and most interesting developments in, for example, Italy and Spain in the thirteenth and fourteenth centuries, and in France in the seventeenth. But it is

1. 251(?)–356.   2. d. 340.   3. 1469–1539.

17

with the third category that this book must be concerned, for it is to this group that the title and office of hermit most properly belongs. Within this definition there was (and is) a wide range of interpretation, and this made for considerable variety.

There was, for example, the *anchorite* attached to a monastery or convent, living the solitary life in his cell, near or within the enclosure. He would be living under rule, and conforming as much as possible to his community's observances. Most communities at some time or other have had solitaries of this kind. Not all anchorites, however, were affiliated to religious orders, for many were 'free-lance', under the direction of the local bishop or his nominee. The anchorage was invariably attached to a church or a religious building where the recluse would be able to assist at Mass, and to receive Holy Communion.

Popular fancy imagines the anchorage to be a tiny room ventilated by a small window and a church-ward 'squint'. This was not so, for in these matters medieval man was both realistic and humane. Nearly all anchorages were big enough to contain two or three rooms, and were surrounded by their own walled gardens. There was a surprising degree of freedom, and there are records of anchoresses having their own servants, receiving visitors, entertaining staying company, and doing a variety of things that show how tolerable and elastic within their limits were the terms of their immurement. They even moved their anchorage on occasion. But it was nonetheless a severe life, and normally the greatest care was taken by ecclesiastical authority to see that only the fit, the self-supporting, and the truly called, were admitted to it by the simple, but dramatically drastic, service that sealed them in for life.

A *hermit* too was licensed to his calling by a service of dedication, but the emphasis was different, and the life to which it admitted even more so. Solitary he might be and remote from habitation in his cell, yet the hermit was not tied to it in the sense the anchorite was. He could roam at will, and often he did. He could move house whenever he wanted, though to do so too often was a bad sign, and might incur ecclesiastical censure and even revocation of the licence. Apart from the ideal of prayer which he shared with the anchorite, the hermit could practise good works impossible to the other and live a totally different sort of life. There are instances of hermits acting as unofficial lighthouse-keepers, in a day when a lighthouse service was unthought of; of hermits keeping bridges in repair, or mending roads, or guarding town gates, or ministering to lepers in lazar-houses, or acting as guides in difficult terrain, or collecting for charity, or being the recognized do-gooder of practical works in a district. There were few things they could not turn their hands to. Basically of course they prayed, and counselled and advised. A hermit could even marry, seemingly without prejudice to his standing, though the terms of his licensing normally carried the requirement that he should live chastely.

For neither anchorite nor hermit was there a shortage of human contact, but obviously one was much more able than the other to make and sustain it. Both were dependent on the charity of their fellow Christians, which in the fourteenth century was readily forthcoming. Probably as many women as men were in reclusion, but hermits were invariably male.

The general practice was, as we have seen, that either form of living was approached by the way of the monastic life. The *Rule* of St Benedict, the father of Western monasticism, specifically provides for this,[4] for from the first it was recognized that it was the discipline learned by living in community which prepared the would-be solitary for the rigour of his new life. But this was not necessarily the case, as the example of Richard Rolle shows. One of the criticisms of Rolle was that he had never submitted to such ordering, but had precipitated himself headlong into the life. Hindsight suggests that he might have written more temperately about the lives of religious and caused less embarrassment

4. *Regula Benedicti*, chapter 1.

to himself and others had he first lived the life he criticized so strongly.

There are anchorites and hermits in all branches of the Catholic Church, though in very small numbers. Public reaction, once it has got over its surprise that such folk still exist, would seem to be a mixture of amused tolerance, complete ignorance, and slightly condescending pity. The medieval world would have understood what it was all about. The ideals of the life were well known, the spiritual benefits both to the solitary and to the community generally were taken for granted, and the totality of self-giving in response to God's call was accepted.

Various reasons have prompted men to retire into a hermitage. The secular priest, aiming at spiritual perfection, might seek it here after years of apostolic labour in a parish. Others might use it as a temporary pick-me-up, living a life of prayer alone for a period, and then returning to parochial work, refreshed and refurbished; there was nothing to prevent them from retiring again into solitude for further strengthening and more service. Some used their hermit vocation as a protest against prevailing clerical laxity, seeking by their own particular witness to challenge others to renewed piety. Some became hermits to expiate their sins. The motives for heeding a call to solitude were many.

There were simpler, more human reasons too to account for the popularity of the solitary life. Medieval life was intolerably public. Towns and villages huddled together for mutual protection and support, and there were very few human functions that could be performed without some eye seeing. To mention but one matter which is probably different from the circumstances of any reader of these notes: everybody slept in the same room, beds (where they existed) could take up to six people, night attire was unknown, and one either slept in one's clothes or in none at all. One can let one's imagination rove widely over this single fact; it will not go far beyond the bounds of possibility. Nor did the parish churches offer a haven of quiet. In addition to their daily religious use they served as the medieval equivalent of a town hall cum community-centre cum parish hall, and within the hallowed walls many different activities were conducted. Justice was administered, courts were convened, contracts made, plays staged, 'church ales' held, and even fairs were accommodated either inside the building or in the churchyard. The whole of life was unbelievably crude and rough for the common man. To sensitive souls the only escape into any sort of privacy must often have seemed an anchorhold somewhere, a hermitage, or a religious house. It is understandable that solitaries were numbered by the hundred in the fourteenth century.

ROLLE THE MYSTIC

Mysticism is a word with various meanings, which accord with the viewpoint of the person using it. Most Christian theologians, however, would subscribe to that given by Dom David Knowles in his *English Mystical Tradition*.[1] We can have knowledge of God, as our Maker and Governor, he says, 'by a natural process of reasoning; this is natural theology. To this we add what Jew and Christian have learnt from God's own revelation of Himself through the inspired writers of scripture, and above all from the words and works of His Son, Jesus Christ.' Beyond these two kinds of knowledge

there is a third by which God and the truths of Christianity can not only be believed and acted upon, but can in varying degrees be directly known and experienced ... This knowledge, this experience, which is never entirely separable from an equally immediate and experimental union with God by love, has three main characteristics. It is recognized by the person concerned as something utterly different from and more real and adequate than all his previous knowledge and love of God. It is experienced as something at once immanent and received, some-

1. pp. 2 and 3.

thing moving and filling the powers of mind and soul. It is felt as taking place at a deeper level of the personality and soul than that on which the normal processes of thought and will take place, and the mystic is aware, both in himself and in others, of the soul, its qualities and of the divine presence and action within it, as something wholly distinct from the reasoning mind with its powers. Finally, this experience is wholly incommunicable, save as a bare statement, and in this respect all the utterances of the mystics are entirely inadequate as representations of the mystical experience, but it brings absolute certainty to the mind of the recipient. This is the traditional mystical theology, the knowledge of God, in its purest form.

As a terse, comprehensive description of what the Church believes about mysticism this could hardly be bettered, though one might wish that the reference to the need for love could have been sharper and more definite. The *sine qua non* of any growth in mystical prayer is a love for God, and a continuing longing for him: without it there can be no union, and indeed the experience can have little abiding significance.

If we look at Rolle's teaching in *The Fire*[2] we will see how closely it agrees with Dom Knowles's criteria, and the editorial rider.

On nearly every page there is an emphasis on the need for loving God and longing after him. Thus, 'there must be a serious intention ... to long continually for the love of God.'[3] 'God the Holy Trinity is to be loved for himself alone.'[4] 'It behoves us to make sure that the love of Christ is in us.'[5] 'No creature can love God too much.'[6] It is unnecessary to multiply instances: in this single work the loving of God is mentioned over 800 times.

Though a great deal of hard work, penance, and ascetic discipline are the required preliminaries for mystical experience, together with the fact that the whole business involves a matter of years rather than hours – Rolle recog-

2. All references to Rolle's doctrine will be drawn from *The Fire*.

3. p. 55.   4. p. 56.   5. p. 61.   6. p. 99.

nizes that there may be exceptions – contemplation itself is
not the fruit of this grind, but is unequivocally the gift of
God. 'It is obvious to those who are in love that no one
attains the heights of devotion at once, or is ravished with
contemplative sweetness. In fact it is only very occasionally
– and then only momentarily – that they are allowed to
experience heavenly things; their progress to spiritual
strength is a gradual one ... perfection is acquired after
great labour.'[7] This finds many echoes throughout the book,
as does the stress that God himself gives the vision. 'No one
can do good, or love God ... unless God enables him to do
so.'[8] 'God infuses them with the calm of holy desires.'[9]
'Wonder seized me that ... God should give me gifts, the
like of which I did not know I could ask for ... from which
I deduce that they are not given for merit, but freely to
whomsoever Christ wills.'[10] 'He shows himself voluntarily to
each man as he wills.'[11] Moreover the contemplative becomes 'aware of a heavenly secret infused into his sweet
love, and known only by himself.'[12] Indeed God himself is
the love which unites the soul to him.[13]

Rolle is clear that he has received this precious gift, for
which he has prepared himself by wholehearted, total, love
for God, and throughout *The Fire* he speaks of the warmth
(physical as well as spiritual), sweetness and melody (both
spiritual) he has enjoyed, and continues to enjoy, as the
result of his contemplative praying. He knows of *locutions* –
for the heavenly harmonies and the celestial choirs are such
– and he has a much heightened sense of the spirit world, if
we are to take his frequent angel references seriously. The
effect of contemplation is joy and wonder beyond power to
describe, and in his struggle to find words he calls it 'intoxicating',[14] 'melting',[15] and 'absorbing'.[16] Yet he still says, 'I
am not adequate to describe even slightly the smallest part
of this joy. For who can describe ineffable fervour? Who
lay bare infinite sweetness?'[17] 'I have to "give up" ... I have

7. p. 51.   8. p. 80.   9. p. 87.   10. p. 93.
11. p. 170.   12. p. 164.   13. p. 105.   14. p. 144.
        15. p. 182.   16. p. 165.   17. p. 150.

not the wit to describe this shout [of joy] or its magnitude, or even the pleasure it gives just to think of it'.[18]

As with other writing mystics Rolle sees that the vision of God makes it impossible to sin. He does not deny that a contemplative may sin, but it cannot happen when he is delighting in God, or is recalling such delight. Theoretically possible, it is most unlikely, for the contemplative 'ought to be willing to lose the great reward of heaven rather than to commit a single sin however venial'. 'Those who love Christ with such fervour ... never ... want to sin again.'[19]

Rolle writes with confidence, and one feels that he knows what he is writing about. It is unfortunate that he had not the benefit of the careful classifications of later centuries, but in spite of this real drawback (as we see it) the warmth, gusto, and evident sincerity of his writings make him the most widely read of all the English masters up to the time of the Reformation.

In the light of all this it is surprising that some modern theologians have criticized and rejected him as a mystic, and would recognize him primarily as a man of letters. His description of contemplation, they say, shows it not to have been on the same pure, high level of those who came after him. That is probably true, even if at times one suspects that the later mystics were speculating where they had not experienced. But one does not restrict the word 'mountaineer' to those who have climbed Mount Everest, nor the word 'mystic' to those whose intellectual appreciation is keener than Rolle's. A mystic by definition is one who has been taken into some sort of deep union with God, and who knows it while he cannot adequately describe it.

One of the difficulties undoubtedly is caused by the temptation to fit the medievals into the categories of later theologians. When, for example, Rolle is speaking of rapture in chapter 37, and distinguishing between 'rapture out of the senses' and 'rapture in the senses' is he describing what St Teresa later taught us to call the *Prayer of Full*

18. p. 153.   19. p. 66.

Union or is it her *Prayer of Quiet*, or what? Rolle explains that being 'rapt out of the senses' means that the person undergoing rapture becomes oblivious to all that goes on around him, unfeeling and unseeing, and presumably (though he does not say so) rigid. This clearly is some form of ecstasy, and so Rolle terms it. The second rapture, which Rolle prefers, is a seizure of the mind only, which leaves the body free and able to cope with circumstances.

According to the Spanish saint the soul in the *Prayer of Full Union* is united to God, not only through the will, but also through all the interior faculties – a highly desirable state according to most experts, though embarrassing to the spectator as well as to the visionary, because neither the times nor the venues of these visitations can be predicted. But is the Englishman referring to the same experience? He disapproves of this particular form of rapture because on occasion it is experienced by evil men too. Maybe he is merely suffering from the lack of modern insight which can distinguish between ecstasies which are physical and those which are psychological or mystical.

At first glance the preferred rapture 'in the senses' looks like the *Prayer of Quiet*, regarded by St Teresa and most teachers since as being on a lower level. It is still super-natural, in that the soul cannot acquire it by its own efforts; only God can produce it. The joys and delights and the sense of the divine presence are indescribable, and produce, for example, 'a love of penance and of crosses, humility and contempt for worldly joys',[20] all of which tally with Rolle But the garment only fits where it touches, and the careful reader of Rolle will find that being 'rapt in the senses' adds up to more than the *Prayer of Quiet*. If we have to squeeze Rolle into a Teresan definition it is more likely that her subsequent distinction (which she seemingly was the first to make) between two forms of Full Union is the right one. One is ecstatic, one non-ecstatic; they are different only in the intensity of the union, not in the essence. In ecstasy the

20. Tanquerey, *The Spiritual Life*, p. 678.

union is much greater.[21] It does not matter very much. Rolle, largely self-taught in the fourteenth century, could not be expected to guess the refinements of the sixteenth.

But there are two other grounds which cause modern disquiet. One is Rolle's stress on the emotional concomitants of contemplation, his warmth (*calor*), sweetness (*dulcor*), and melody (*canor*).[22] The other is the absence of any reference to the bitter spiritual experience generally known as 'the dark night', or to the higher levels of contemplative prayer. Something may be said in Rolle's defence.

(1) That there is a place for emotion in religious experience few would care to deny. Yet the continuing denigration of it since the time of St John of the Cross is no help to some who are engaged in the mystic quest. There are real dangers, too obvious to describe, in unbridled, uncriticized emotion, but it does seem that for some (though not all) in their closely integrated personality the deep awareness of the presence of God in their inmost spirit expresses itself in physical and mental ways. They are joyful and *feel* joyful. Richard Rolle is one such person. He is not unique in feeling physical heat as the result of spiritual experience. On one occasion Ste Thérèse de Lisieux experienced something similar. She felt herself 'suddenly pierced with a dart of fire.... I cannot explain this transport, nor can any comparison express the intensity of this flame. It seemed to me that an invisible force immersed me completely in fire.'[23]

A Western Christian discovers to his surprise that the Orthodox Church both expects and encourages a physical reaction to mystical prayer. Unless one is prepared to dismiss the Easterns as being incapable of this sort of prayer, then Rolle gets powerful support from them. A quotation taken almost at random from the recent Orthodox anthology, *The Art of Prayer*,[24] will show this. The

21. Guibert, *The Theology of the Spiritual Life*, p. 333.
22. Chapters 14 and 15.
23. Quoted in Evelyn Underhill's introduction to Miss Comper's *Fire of Love*, p. xvii.
24. London, 1966.

26

writer, Theophan the Recluse, is writing of the *Jesus Prayer.*[25]

How does the *Jesus Prayer* help us in this? Through the feeling of warmth which develops in and around the heart as the effect of this prayer. The habit of prayer is not formed suddenly, but requires long work and toil. The *Jesus Prayer*, and the warmth which accompanies it, helps better than anything else in the formation of the habit of prayer.

The question now arises whether this warmth is spiritual. No, it is *not* spiritual. It is ordinary physical warmth. But since it keeps the attention of the mind in the heart, and thus helps the development there of the spiritual movements described earlier, it is called spiritual – provided that it is not accompanied by sensual pleasure, however slight, but keeps the soul and body in sober mood.

Theophan is quite alive to the dangers of false emotions and warns against them. The point is that, like most other Orthodox theologians, he allows them a proper and even prominent place in spiritual development. No Orthodox is surprised that the writer in the *Way of a Pilgrim,*[26] addicted as he is to the *Jesus Prayer*, finds his heart grow warm, physically warm, as he offers this prayer over and over again. Rolle's devotion to the Holy Name, a practice which he never fails to commend to others, suggests that his own experience, uninfluenced by Greek ascetic theology, is a demonstration beyond reasonable doubt that for some, if not for all, a burning love for our Lord, with the frequent repetition of his Name, produces psychosomatic reactions. The two other strong characteristics of Rolle's praying, sweetness[27] and melody, have no physical expression, and must be understood as basically spiritual.

25. A devotion to the Name of Our Lord. In practice it is the continual repetition of the sentence, 'Lord Jesus Christ, Son of God, have mercy on me, a sinner.'

26. A very famous Russian book of spirituality written by an anonymous pilgrim.

27. The frequent, and to modern ears rather irritating, references to 'sweetness' must be seen in the contemporary setting. In Rolle's

(2) Not unrelated to the matter of 'feelings' is the 'dark night'. This desolating time has been variously named by Western theologians, but basically all are agreed that it is a period of purgation in which the senses and the spirit are cleansed of every shred of self-interest so that God, and God alone, and God wholly, is the concern of the mystic. The pain that this stripping causes can be very grievous indeed, and may last for a long time, for the soul is generally embedded in the world and in its self-interest. This 'night' which makes the soul live by a faith that is stark and naked, yet does not quench its persistent longing for God, is not unbroken gloom. For when God wills the clouds part, and a ray of ineffable light streams out, to illumine for a moment the countryside, the goal, and the pilgrim himself. Then the clouds close in again, and the journey plods onward and upward. There is very little of the honeyed sweetness, heat and melody which continually excite Rolle, but rather a very great deal of hard slog over difficult terrain, through fog and dark, and at times without any awareness of a Presence at hand to help. But when the purgation is over the reward is apparently fantastic. It cannot be described, alas, for those who are there or nearly there know no words to tell of the humanly untellable. But outwardly one can discern a certainty of God, a serenity, a beauty, a humility, a rock-likeness, which are strangely impressive and attractive.

But Rolle in his buoyancy bypasses this purgative discipline. His occasional references to toil and labour do not amount to recognition of its need. For him it does not seem to exist. He is not necessarily wrong, though to Western eyes his doctrine may appear lopsided.

The Orthodox Church, again a salutary check in these matters, knows nothing of dark nights, though obviously some of her spiritual giants have endured them. But as a

---

day sweetness was highly valued because of its comparative rarity. People knew nothing of sugar cane, sugar beet, or saccharin. Such sweetening as they had came from honey.

whole the Eastern masters do not experience them. Their understanding of God is such that they do not expect this sort of darkness, and so do not have it. Rolle is, all unwittingly, surprisingly Eastern in his approach, and his exuberance, always to be looked at critically as well as sympathetically, still acts as a corrective to later austerities which sometimes are deemed essential. Clearly for some 'the King's way of the Holy Cross' is so counterbalanced by 'the joy that is set before them' that they attend but little to the hardness of the way. For them it must be Rolle: it could not be Walter Hilton, *The Cloud of Unknowing*, or St John of the Cross.[28]

SHORTER NOTES

Alliterative Artifice

This simple Introduction does not warrant a discussion on the author's Latinity and style. It has been called 'polyphonic prose', and many-voiced it is indeed. In both languages Rolle makes full use of various literary devices: assonance, antithesis, balance, rhyme, rhythm, and, above all, alliteration. This last feature, outstandingly characteris-

28. Evelyn Underhill (*Mysticism*, p. 318), writing of the *Prayer of Quiet*, made a distinction between types of mystics which seems valid for all stages of prayer. 'In its description, all mystics will be found to lean to one side or the other, to the affirmative or negative element which it contains. The austere mysticism of Eckhart and his followers, their temperamental sympathy with the Neoplatonic language of Dionysius the Areopagite, caused them to describe it – and also very often the highest state of contemplation to which it leads – as above all things an emptiness, a divine dark, an ecstatic deprivation. They will not profane its deep satisfactions by the inadequate terms proper to earthly peace and joy: and, true to their school, fall back on the paradoxically suggestive powers of negation. To St Teresa, and mystics of her type, on the other hand, even a little and inadequate image of its joy seems better than none. To them it is a sweet calm, a gentle silence, in which the lover apprehends the presence of the Beloved: a God-given state, over which the self has little control.'

tic of his writings, must be mentioned, for it disappears completely in translation. The medievals thought highly of this practice, and indulged it frequently. Clearly Rolle shared their view; his works, whether Latin or English, provide examples in plenty of his skill in this direction.

The *Incendium* is full of them. Here are two from chapter five: even if the reader has no Latin he will be able to appreciate the mastery Rolle exhibited in this literary medium:

Peccatores lugebunt quando pauperes portabuntur ad pacem perhennem et delectabuntur in deliciis deitatis vivificantis, Christi vultum veraciter videntes, qui venusti erant virtutibus et in fervore spirituali feliciter floruerunt quamvis cum sublimibus huius seculi nequaquam sumpserunt solacium, nec inter sapientes insanos seminaverunt superbiam, sed sustinuerunt angariam ab iniquis, et temptaciones exterminaverunt a throno Trinitatis ut in tranquilitate tenerentur.[1]

Hinc est utique quod sine merore moriuntur, immo cum gaudio gradientes ad tam grandem gradum elevantur in eternis honoribus, et consistunt coronati in copiosissima Creatoris contemplacione, concinentes cum choris clarissimis, qui eciam ardencius anhelant in essenciam ipsam omnibus imperantem.[2]

If modern taste finds this practice generally unacceptable, what would it make of the *Melos Amoris*, which because of its excessive alliteration is tedious to read and impossible to translate – but for a still young Rolle great fun to write?

Frustra fundantur falsi fideles quia funditus finietur fiducia fenerantis, et fumo inferni ficti ferientur et omnes utique umbra honoris operti ut appareant in aulis avaris. Fervebunt fetentes formidine futura; formosus et fortis in feno falluntur et ideo imbuti impio instinctu fervore felici numquam fruentur quia federati fuerunt in factis falsorum ut fixi in fervore finiendi favoris feruntur cum furibus facibus frementes: horum fornax fetidus fauces iam fringet, nam fugiunt fidem famamque fugant; sic filii feroces formantur fortiter ut fundum furencium penetrent post pauca et penas percipiant perpetuo perdurantes. (*Melos Amoris,* chapter 17).

It is difficult to avoid the impression that at times Rolle is so 'inebriated with the exuberance of his own verbosity' that his alliterations have obscured his thought – and made life unnecessarily hard for the reader. It would not be true, however, to say that he is merely playing with words, for nearly always they have some bearing on his theme, remotely if not directly. But it is a bad habit in a serious writer, restricting and exaggerating. Rolle never freed himself from it, and presumably never wanted to; in any case the medievals admired it.

Rolle's Englishness

Despite the existence of four outstanding English mystics of the fourteenth century, there is nothing that would justify their being classified as an 'English School'. They were all highly individual in their approach, and though it could be said that in fundamental doctrine they do not contradict each other – except on those occasions when Hilton and *The Cloud of Unknowing* warn against an emotionalism of Rolle's type – it cannot be truthfully asserted that they depend on or develop each other.

They have certain superficial characteristics in common, however. Their individualism expressed itself not only in their mystical approach but also in their manner of life, for they all had to do with the solitary life. Rolle was a hermit, Mother Julian an anchoress, *The Cloud* was written by one recluse for another, and Walter Hilton wrote primarily for solitaries, and is thought to have been one himself.

Also, much of what they wrote was in the vernacular. This was a new thing, due partly to the fact that some of their works were written for religious women, but due primarily to the changing pattern of national life when at last English was coming into its own as a respectable and worthy channel of communication. In the writings of each there are splendid passages in the mother tongue, revealing not only their mastery of it, but also its complete adequacy for expressing the deepest truths hitherto hidden beneath the Latin.

But there is also a robust note of common sense about them all, not least in Rolle. Of the four he would seem the most unlikely to champion moderation, for he was an enthusiast with a sharply defined sense of right and wrong, and with a poet's eye and power of expression. But he is as balanced as any, and this is a factor to be remembered when assessing his teaching. Whether he is writing English or Latin matters little: there is the same note of caution against excess. In *The Fire*, for example, he says some very wise things about fasting. No fanatic could have written this:

> Yet the abstinence in which he [the contemplative] lives should not be excessive, nor on the other hand should he display too much extravagance. ... The true lover of Christ, one who is taught by him, does not worry overmuch whether there is too much or too little. ... I myself have eaten and drunk things that are considered delicacies; not because I love such dainties, but in order to sustain my being in the service of God, and in the joy of Christ. For his sake I conformed quite properly to those with whom I was living lest I should invent a sanctity where none existed.[1]

This moderation is typical of *The Fire of Love*, with the exception of one outstanding instance. Like many medievals and celibates he regards women as a sex with the gravest doubt and suspicion. Most of his writings exhibit this quirk. In *The Fire* he makes no bones about it. He refers to the danger explicitly in many places (chapters 23, 24, and 30, will serve for example) and implicitly in such phrases as 'carnal pleasures', 'worldly corruption', 'flesh', 'worldly vanity', and the like. It seems to be always at the back of his mind. Yet at one time, faithfully reported in chapter 12, he showed an undue familiarity towards four of them, and one by one their merited rebukes warned him off effectively and enduringly. Offsetting his harshness and fear it must be recalled that in his maturity he directed faith-

1. pp. 77–8.

fully and well the anchoress, Margaret Kirkby, and acted as if he were chaplain to the nuns at Hampole Convent.[2] His early bark was worse than his mellowed bite.

Genuine Writings

Rolle was a prolific writer and has left behind him a large body of works recognizably his, both in Latin and English. Such was his influence and popularity that he has been credited with many other writings not so certainly from his pen. Much research has been given to the matter, and the great authority of the American scholar, Miss Hope Emily Allen, gives as his genuine writings, and in some cases their conjectured dates, the following:

Early Works: *Canticum Amoris* (before 1322); *Judica me, Deus* (before 1322); *Melos Amoris* (1326/7); *Job* (1327/ 30); *Canticles* (before 1330).

Scriptural Commentaries: *Super Threnos*; *Super Apocalypsim*; *Super Orationem Dominicam*; *Super Symbolum Apostolorum*; *Super Mulierem Fortem*. (All these are thought to have been written before 1340, and after 1330.)

Commentaries on the Psalter: *De Dei Misericordia*; *Latin Psalter* (early, about 1327/30); *Super Psalmum XXm.*
(Everything so far has been in Latin, but now he begins to write in English as well.)

2. Was he ordained by then? There is no record of his having received Holy Orders, though his later writings sometimes read as though he were a priest. Dr Hodgson, who once committed herself to the belief that Rolle was always a layman, later retracted, influenced by the French scholar, Dom Maurice Noetinger. In *The Month* for January, 1926, he quotes a sentence from the *Melos Amoris* which seems to imply priestly status: 'nisi sanguinem Salvatoris mihi in subsidium semper sumpsissem' which means 'unless I had always received the Saviour's Blood for my strengthening'. In the fourteenth century layfolk no longer received the chalice, nor indeed did they often go to Holy Communion at all. (G. Hodgson, *Office Psalms*, 1931.)

Super Magnificat (in Latin and English); *English Psalter* (1340/49); *Psalms 90 and 91* (English).

Latin Treatises: *Contra Amatores Mundi*; *Incendium Amoris* (1343); *Emendatio Vitae*.

English Epistles: *Ego Dormio* (English, despite its traditional title – 1343); *The Comandment*; *The Form of Living* (1348/9).

Short English Prose Pieces: *The Bee*; *Desyre and Delit*; *Gastly Gladnesse* (after 1343); *The Seven Gifts of the Holy Spirit*; *English Commentary on the Ten Commandments*; *Meditations on the Passion*.

Miscellaneous English Lyrics.

With this list the English expert, Dr Geraldine Hodgson, would be in broad agreement, but with her greater sympathy she would accept as genuine some works over which Miss Allen had reservations.

Books by, and about, Rolle

Though Richard Rolle enjoyed a considerable vogue in the early years of this century, few of the books which then popularized him have survived in print. It is perhaps time that his image was refurbished and his work reassessed. Most of the books below can be obtained without difficulty through local library services.

Richard Rolle's Writings

C. HORSTMANN, *Yorkshire Writers* (Richard Rolle of Hampole and his followers), two volumes, London, 1895. From this work stems our current interest in Rolle. By no means have all of Horstmann's theories proved acceptable to modern scholars.

M. DEANESLEY, *Incendium Amoris*, London, 1915.

R. MISYN, *The Fire of Love and the Mending of Life*,

London, 1896. This translation was made in the fifteenth century.

F. M. COMPER, *The Fire of Love and the Mending of Life*, London, 1914. This is a gentle modernization of Misyn's text.

G. HODGSON, *The Form of Perfect Living, and other Treaties*, London, 1910.

Minor Works of Richard Rolle, London, 1923.

Rolle and 'Our Daily Work', London, 1929.

Richard Rolle's Version of the Penitential Psalms, London, 1928.

H. L. HUBBARD, *The Mending of Life*, London, 1922. A modern English version.

M. NOETINGER, *Le Feu de l'Amour, Le Modèle de la Vie Parfaite, Le Pater*, Tours, 1928.

E. F. J. ARNOULD, *The Melos Amoris of Richard Rolle of Hampole*, Oxford, 1957.

G. C. HESELTINE, *The Fire of Love*, London, 1935. A modern translation.

Selections from Rolle's Writings

G. C. HESELTINE, *Selected Works of Richard Rolle*, London, 1930.

J. G. HARRELL, *Selected Writings of Richard Rolle*, London, 1963.

Books about Rolle

The York Breviary, Surtees Society, volume 75, ii, appendix v, London, 1882. This gives the Latin text of the *Legenda*, a translation of which will be found in Miss Comper's book below.

H. E. ALLEN, *Writings ascribed to Richard Rolle*, New York, 1927.

English Writings of Richard Rolle, Oxford, 1931.

G. HODGSON, *The Sanity of Mysticism*, London, 1926.
These two ladies are the acknowledged authorities on

Rolle. The diligent and untiring labours of Miss Allen produced what is by common consent the most complete reference book on the hermit, and no serious student can afford to ignore it. It is almost magisterial, but it has to be read with caution, as Miss Allen tends to treat her often brilliant conjectures as if they were facts, and to go on from there. She may well be right in most cases, but not in all. Dr Hodgson, too, has a great devotion to Rolle, and her scholarly insight may be thought a little safer than Miss Allen's intuitions.

F. M. COMPER, *The Life and Lyrics of Richard Rolle*, London, 1928. Still the best introduction to Rolle, despite some inaccuracies.

Background Reading

Most books which have to do with Christian mysticism give Rolle generous treatment. The books listed below do, with the exception of the last four, which are 'background' only.

E. UNDERHILL, *Mysticism*, London, 1911.

P. RENAUDIN, *Quatre Mystiques Anglais*, Paris, 1945.

R. PETRY, ed., *Late Medieval Mysticism*, London, 1957.

C. PEPLER, *The English Religious Heritage*, London, 1958.

D. KNOWLES, *The English Mystical Tradition*, London, 1961.

G. SITWELL, *Medieval Spiritual Writers*, London, 1961.

M. THORNTON, *English Spirituality*, London, 1963.

J. WALSH, *Pre-Reformation English Spirituality*, London, no date.

R. H. BENSON, *A Book of the Love of Jesus*, London, 1906.

F. A. PATTERSON, *The Middle English Penitential Lyric*, New York, 1966.

(These two books contain poems by Rolle.)

R. M. CLAY, *The Hermits and Anchorites of England*, London, 1914.

F. D. S. DARWIN, *The English Medieval Recluse*, London, no date.

Introduction

J. LECLERCQ, ed., *La Spiritualité du Moyen Âge*, Liguge, 1961.

MORRIS BISHOP, *Middle Ages*, London, 1968.

Pronunciation

It is sometimes asked how the surname *Rolle* is pronounced. Most people call it 'roll' as if it were a piece of bread. Others rhyme it with 'dollar', believing that each syllable was sounded and that the 'o' was short in medieval times. An opinion received from the appropriate department of Newcastle University suggests that either could be right, but that the former is more probable: 'Conservative speakers would give it two syllables, but in that part of the country [Yorkshire] it would be more likely to have one syllable with a long vowel.'

ACKNOWLEDGEMENTS

The Latin text behind this translation is that which belongs to Emmanuel College, Cambridge (MS 35), corrected and certified by John Newton, Vicar-general and Treasurer of York. When he made his emendations is not known, but it must have been before his death in 1414. Miss Margaret Deanesley published this text in 1915, and her book is essential for anyone seeking to study the *Incendium Amoris* seriously.

Most of the books listed above have contributed in some degree or other to this one, but the translator is indebted in particular to four people who have helped prepare *The Fire*. The Abbot of Nashdom found time to read most of the manuscript and to make many and helpful suggestions, besides making the Abbey library freely available. He is in no way responsible for any errors herein. Joyce (*sponsa carissima*) and John Wolters read it all patiently and critically, and reduced many solecisms to English. Both shared in the revisionary typing. The great bulk of the typing was done by Audrey Bolton, generous in her time and labour, and skilled in interpreting an illegible script. The librarians of Newcastle City Library obtained from widely different sources every book that was asked for, all of which were out of print and otherwise unprocurable. To all these the editor would express his sincere gratitude.

C.C.W.   Newcastle upon Tyne, 1970

THE FIRE OF LOVE

CHAPTER HEADINGS

These were added later by an unknown hand. They follow the natural divisions of the book.

41

PROLOGUE

I CANNOT tell you how surprised I was the first time I felt
my heart begin to warm. It was real warmth too, not
imaginary, and it felt as if it were actually on fire. I was
astonished at the way the heat surged up, and how this new
sensation brought great and unexpected comfort. I had to
keep feeling my breast to make sure there was no physical
reason for it! But once I realized that it came entirely from
within, that this fire of love had no cause, material or sinful,
but was the gift of my Maker, I was absolutely delighted,
and wanted my love to be even greater. And this longing
was all the more urgent because of the delightful effect and
the interior sweetness which this spiritual flame fed into
my soul. Before the infusion of this comfort I had never
thought that we exiles could possibly have known such
warmth, so sweet was the devotion it kindled. It set my soul
aglow as if a real fire was burning there.

Yet as some may well remind us, there are people on fire
with love for Christ, for we can see how utterly they despise
the world, and how wholly they are given over to the
service of God. If we put our finger near a fire we feel
the heat; in much the same way a soul on fire with love
feels, I say, a genuine warmth. Sometimes it is more, sometimes less: it depends on our particular capacity.

What mortal man could survive that heat at its peak – as
we can know it, even here – if it persisted? He must inevitably wilt before the vastness and sweetness of love so per-
fervid, and heat so indescribable. Yet at the same time he is
bound to long eagerly for just this to happen: to breathe
his soul out, with all its superb endowment of mind, in this
honeyed flame, and, quit of this world, be held in thrall
with those who sing their Maker's praise.

But some things are opposed to charity: carnal, sordid
things which beguile a mind at peace. And sometimes in

this bitter exile physical need and strong human affection obtrude into this warmth, to disturb and quench this flame (which metaphorically I call 'fire', because it burns and enlightens). They cannot take away what is irremovable, of course, because this is something which has taken hold of my heart. Yet because of these things this cheering warmth is for a while absent. It will reappear in time, though until it does I am going to be spiritually frozen, and because I am missing what I have become accustomed to, will feel myself bereft. It is then that I want to recapture that awareness of inner fire which my whole being, physical as well as spiritual, so much approves; with it it knows itself to be secure.

Nowadays I find that even sleep ranges itself against me! The only spare time I have is that which I am obliged to give to slumber. When I am awake I can try to warm my soul up, though it is numb with cold. For I know how to kindle it when the soul is settled in devotion and how to raise it above earthly things with overwhelming desire. But this eternal and overflowing love does not come when I am relaxing, nor do I feel this spiritual ardour when I am tired out after, say, travelling; nor is it when I am absorbed with worldly interests, or engrossed in never-ending arguments. At times like these I catch myself growing cold: cold until once again I put away all things external, and make a real effort to stand in my Saviour's presence: only then do I abide in this inner warmth.

I offer, therefore, this book for the attention, not of the philosophers and sages of this world, not of great theologians bogged down in their interminable questionings, but of the simple and unlearned, who are seeking rather to love God than to amass knowledge. For he is not known by argument, but by what we do and how we love. I think that while the matters contained in such questionings are the most demanding of all intellectually, they are much less important when the love of Christ is under consideration. Anyhow they are impossible to understand! So I have not written for the experts, unless they have forgotten and put behind them all those things that belong to the world; unless now they are eager to surrender to a longing for God.

To achieve this however they must, first, fly from every worldly honour; they must hate all vainglory and the parade of knowledge. And then, conditioned by great poverty, through prayer and meditation they can devote themselves to the love of God. It will not be surprising if then an inner spark of the uncreated charity should appear to them and prepare their hearts for the fire which consumes everything that is dark, and raises them to that pitch of ardour which is so lovely and pleasant. Then will they pass beyond the things of time, and sit enthroned in infinite peace. The more learned they are, the more ability they naturally have for loving, always provided of course that they both despise themselves, and rejoice to be despised by others. And so, because I would stir up by these means every man to love God, and because I am trying to make plain the ardent nature of love and how it is supernatural, the title selected for this book will be *The Fire of Love.*

CHAPTER 1

Man's conversion to God, and matters that help or hinder his conversion.

EVERYONE who lives in this deplorable exile of ours knows that he cannot be filled with a love of eternity, or anointed with the sweet oil of heaven, unless he be truly converted to God. Before he can experience even a little of God's love he must really be turned to him, and, in mind at least, be wholly turned from every earthly thing. The turning indeed is a matter of duly ordered love, so that, first, he loves what he ought to love and not what he ought not, and, second, his love kindles more towards the former than to the latter. God is to be loved, of course, most of all: heavenly things too are to be much loved; but little love, or at least no more than is necessary, may be given to earthly things. This surely is the way a man turns to Christ: to desire nothing but him. To turn away from those 'good things' of the world, which pervert rather than protect those who love them, involves the withering of physical lust and the hatred of wickedness of any sort. So you will find there are people who have no taste for earthly things, and who deal with mundane matters no more than is absolutely necessary.

Because those who amass fortunes find comfort in such things – they do not know who will ultimately reap the benefit! – they are not therefore entitled to enjoy even a little cheerful, comforting, heavenly love. Yet they reckon they have had already some experience of future bliss – at least they say so – because of their devotion, a devotion which is feigned, and not genuinely holy. But surely it is this graceless presumption that will bring about their downfall, for their love for earthly treasure is unlimited. What is more, they will fall from the sweetness with which God delights his lovers. All love which is not God-directed

48

is bad love, and makes its possessors bad too. And this is the reason why those who love worldly splendour with an evil love catch fire of a different sort, and separate themselves ever further from the fire of divine love, further in fact than the distance separating highest heaven from lowest earth! Indeed such people become like what they love, for they take their tone from the greed of their day and age. Because they will not give up their old ways they come to prefer life's specious emptiness to the warmth of happiness. They exchange the glory of incorruptible charity for a fleeting lust of 'beauty'. And this they could not possibly do were they not blinded by a counterfeit 'fire of love', which both devastates virtue at its source, and encourages vice in its growth.

Yet on the other hand there are many who, because they care nothing for feminine beauty or riotous living, reckon therefore that they will be sure of salvation. Because of this chastity, outward and visible, they see themselves as saints standing out from the rest. But this is a wrong and silly assumption if they are not at the same time destroying the real root of sin, greed. As the Bible says, there is nothing worse than the love of money,[1] for it means that one's heart is everlastingly bothering about the love of the transitory, and not giving itself a chance to acquire devotion. Love for God and love for the world cannot coexist in the same soul : the stronger drives out the weaker, and it soon appears who loves the world, and who follows Christ. The strength of people's love is shown in what they do. The lovers of Christ set themselves against the world and the flesh, just as those who love the world oppose God and their own soul.

The elect of God, indeed, eat and drink 'in God', and all their thinking is directed Godwards; they attend to mundane matters only as need – not lust – may require. They have to talk of earthly things of course, but they do so with reluctance, and they never dwell thereon. Mentally they turn back to God with all speed, and spend the rest of the time with divine duties. They neither loaf nor gad about

1. 1 Timothy 6 : 10.

49

after the spectacular or the frivolous – the mark of the reprobate! – for they sincerely care for the things which belong to God. Nor are they backward in speaking about these things, or doing them, or meditating upon them.

The reprobate on the other hand regard the things of God altogether too casually. His word they hear inattentively, their prayers they offer without love, their meditations are made without pleasure. Admittedly they go to church and even pack it to the doors: they beat their breasts and heave great sighs, but none of this means a thing. Seen of men they may be; heard of God they are not. While they are physically in the house of God, mentally they are miles away, thinking of the worldly goods they possess or would like to have, their hearts far from God. They eat and drink, not because they need to, but because they want to, and in sex and food they find all their enjoyment and pleasure. They give bread in plenty to the poor, and perhaps will clothe the cold with a coat, but all the time they are doing their alms in mortal sin, for show. Certainly when they do these things with means unjustly gotten, it is not surprising that they do not please their Redeemer, but rather provoke their Judge to vengeance.

Just as the elect of God, when they are seeing to the needs of the world or of the body, direct their thoughts Godwards, so the reprobate, when they seem to be serving God, are inwardly thinking of the world and things which have to do with worldly or carnal greed. And just as the elect in the relief of need do not grieve God, so the reprobate seemingly busy with good deeds do not please him, because they adulterate their good deeds with bad.

The devil has got hold of many whom we count good. For he possesses those who are merciful, chaste, and humble – self-confessed sinners to a man, of coursé, hairshirted and penance-laden! Very often indeed are mortal wounds obscured by the odour of sanctity. He has the busy worker, the compelling preacher, but not, surely, the man whose heart is aglow with charity, ever eager to love God and indifferent to vanity. The eager love of the wicked on the other hand is for what is shameful. They have ceased from all spiritual exercise, or at least are flabby and very feeble. Their love has no pattern, being given more to things temporal than eternal, more to bodies than to souls.

CHAPTER 2

No one attains supreme devotion quickly, or is refreshed by the sweetness of contemplation.

IT is obvious to those who are in love that no one attains the heights of devotion at once, or is ravished with contemplative sweetness. In fact it is only very occasionally – and then only momentarily – that they are allowed to experience heavenly things; their progress to spiritual strength is a gradual one. When they have attained the gravity of behaviour so necessary and have achieved a certain stability of mind – as much as changing circumstances permit – a certain perfection is acquired after great labour. It is then that they can feel some joy in loving God.

Notwithstanding, it appears that all those who are mighty performers in virtue immediately and genuinely experience the warmth of uncreated or created charity, melt in the immense fire of love, and sing within their hearts the song of divine praise. For this mystery is hidden from the many, and is revealed to the few, and those the most special. So the more sublime such a level is, the fewer – in this world – are those who find it. Rarely in fact have we found a man who is so holy or even perfect in this earthly life endowed with love so great as to be raised up to contemplation to the level of jubilant song. This would mean that he would receive within himself the sound that is sung in heaven, and that he would echo back the praises of God as it were in harmony, pouring forth sweet notes of music and composing spiritual songs as he offers his heavenly praises, and that he would truly experience in his heart the genuine fire of the love of God. It would be surprising if anyone without such experience should claim the name of contemplative when the psalmist, speaking in character as the typical contemplative, exclaims, *I will go into the house of the Lord, with the voice of praise and thanksgiving.*[1] The praise, of course, is the praise offered by the banqueter, one who is feeding on heavenly sweetness.

Further, perfect souls who have been caught up into this friendship – surpassing, abundant, and eternal! – discover that life is suffused with imperishable sweetness from the glittering chalice of sweet charity. In holy happy wisdom they inhale joyful heat into their souls, and as a result are much cheered by the indescribable comfort of God's healing medicine. Here at all events is refreshment for those who love their high and eternal heritage, even though in their earthly exile distress befell them. However they think it not unfitting to endure a few years' hardship in order to be raised to heavenly thrones, and never leave them. They have been selected out of all mankind to be the beloved of their Maker and to be crowned with glory, since, like the seraphim in highest heaven, they have been inflamed with the same love. Physically they may have sat in solitary state, but in mind they have companied with angels, and have yearned for their Beloved. Now they sing most sweetly a prayer of love everlasting as they rejoice in Jesus:

O honeyed flame, sweeter than all sweet, delightful beyond all creation!

My God, my Love, surge over me, pierce me by your love, wound me with your beauty.

Surge over me, I say, who am longing for your comfort.

Reveal your healing medicine to your poor lover.

See, my one desire is for you; it is you my heart is seeking.

My soul pants for you; my whole being is athirst for you.

Yet you will not show yourself to me; you look away; you bar the door, shun me, pass me over;

You even laugh at my innocent sufferings.

1. Psalms 42:4.

And yet you snatch your lovers away from all earthly
    things.
You lift them above every desire for worldly matters.
You make them capable of loving you –
    and love you they do indeed.
So they offer you their praise in spiritual song
    which bursts out from that inner fire;
    they know in truth the sweetness of the dart of love.
Ah, eternal and most lovable of all joys,
    you raise us from the very depths,
    and entrance us with the sight of divine majesty so
    often!
Come into me, Beloved!
All ever I had I have given up for you;
    I have spurned all that was to be mine,
    that you might make your home in my heart,
    and I your comfort.
Do not forsake me now, smitten with such great longing,
    whose consuming desire is to be amongst those who
    love you.
Grant me to love you,
    to rest in you,
    that in your kingdom I may be worthy
    to appear before you world without end.

CHAPTER 3

Every one who is chosen has his state ordered by God.

THOSE contemplatives who are most on fire with the love
of eternity are like those higher beings whose eagerness for
eternal love is most enjoyable and outstanding. They never,
or scarcely ever, engage in outside activity, or accept the
dignity of ecclesiastical preferment or rank. They tend to
keep themselves to themselves, ever ready to reach up to
Christ with joyful song. In this respect the Church is following the angelic hierarchy, for the supernal angels are

not sent out on errands, but attend closely to God. Similarly the masters of contemplative love give themselves to the things of God, and not to lording it over people. Such matters are reserved for those more concerned for that kind of activity, but less interested in spiritual delight.

Each of God's chosen has his fore-appointed place. That one may have been chosen for advancement, while this is striving to surrender himself wholly to God; God within him is drawing him, and so everything outside is ignored. Such folk are holy indeed, though men in general rate them pretty low, since they rarely go out of their way to do miracles: they prefer rather to remain in interior solitude.

And there are those who quite properly give themselves to serve God in other people, and who control those under them with sensitivity.

Again to others who live lives of unsuspected discipline there are sometimes granted – and made known – 'signs', even before they die; or it may be after death when perhaps they themselves for some period are enduring the sharp afflictions of purgatory! Not every saint does, or has done, a miracle before his death or after; nor, on the other hand, does every reprobate lack one! The judgement of God is hidden indeed. Evil men become worse when they see miracles wrought by sinners; on the other hand, the goodness of those who hold lightly to the things which can be indifferently good or bad increases more and more in the love of their Maker. Admittedly some evil men have done works that are good, but from them they have looked for the praise of men, not of God. When they die, these things die too, for they have had what they were wanting here on earth. It often happens that those whose goodness is second-rate and less than perfect work miracles, but for the most part it is the outstanding ones who now rest wholly in the heavenly places before the Face of God, having their reward amongst the great angelic choirs. This lies behind the special dignity attaching to the Feast of St Michael who is not generally reckoned to belong to one of the top orders of angels. So there are certain people who, though they are converted to God and are penitent and have forsaken the affairs of the world, rejoice in the thought that after death their name may be honoured by those who follow them. A faithful servant of Christ, of course, pays no attention to such matters lest he lose all he is working for.

Things common to good and evil alike are not to be sought by God's holy ones, unless it means that charity and spiritual virtues are being planted in our hearts. For these not only keep the soul from the corruption of sin but, at the Judgement, will transform the body too into something for ever memorable. Things done here on earth soon perish, but there they persist for ever – in honour or in confusion! Men of action and rank, even if they are outstanding for their virtue or knowledge, should always put contemplatives before themselves, reckoning them to be their superiors before God, and admitting that they themselves are not capable of contemplation unless, maybe, God's grace should inspire them to it.

CHAPTER 4

The difference between God's lovers and the world's; their rewards.

A HUMAN soul cannot know the fire of eternal love unless first he has completely cut adrift from worldly vanity of every kind. There must be a serious intention to study heavenly things, to long continually for the love of God, and to give every creature its due meed of affection. For if it is for God's sake that we love everything, we love God in it rather than the thing itself. And so we rejoice, not in it but in God – in whom, indeed, we shall glory and rejoice for ever. But evil men are out to enjoy this present world, and they make it the object of their love: they are always seeking things to do with worldly pleasure. What greater folly, more pitiful and damning, can anyone show than to cling to things which are by their very nature passing and decaying?

For God the Holy Trinity is to be loved for himself alone. To the triune God let us give our whole mind: let us strive to relate all our thinking to him as its term: that he may be glorified in us for ever and ever. Our very selves, and all those others whom we love, we love for him alone.

The sinner lies who says he loves God, and yet has no qualms about serving sin. For everyone who loves God is free, and in no servitude to sin. For such a man controls himself, and is steadfast in the serving of righteousness. It is when we love earthly things and earthly comforts for their own sake that we show clearly that we are not loving God. If in this way we make creatures our delight we are to be reckoned not as his servants but as his enemies. We are setting things above their Creator, and caring nothing for the desire and pursuit of things eternal. Surely it is a dreadful moment for the soul (and a sign of everlasting perdition!) when a man surrenders himself wholly to the world, and deliberately gives himself over to the lust of the flesh, and error of every kind. Small wonder that the poor wretch's destruction begins while he is living with his pleasures. While he is thinking about wallowing in his lusts, he is hurrying on to everlasting punishment in hell!

Let no one then dare presume, or boast about his prowess; further, let him not defend himself when contempt and insults and obloquy are heaped upon him. He must not return an evil word for evil, but accept everything with equanimity: praise and insult alike. If in fact we do behave like this we shall rejoice in Christ for ever – it being understood of course that we are loving him here all the time and ardently. Our love for him, rooted in our hearts and steadfast, changes us into his own likeness, and with its fiery love feeds into our minds a glory of another sort, one which is divine.

For his love is a fire which sets our hearts aflame so that they glow and burn; and it purges them from all the foulness of sin. This fire blazes in his chosen ones, and makes them (in mind at least) look heavenwards, and to long ceaselessly for the release of death. Meanwhile, so long as there exists a possibility of our sinning, let us set our minds to flee from worldly prosperity, and cheerfully put up with hardship. The evil mind is perishing even in the midst of its joys; it is destroying itself with attractive poison as it searches for happiness in created things. We must try to avoid this contagion by maintaining our appetite for the spiritual nourishment that is reserved in heaven for fiery lovers.

Thus, with Christ's consent, let us find consolation in the songs of love, and take our delight in the sweetness of devotion. In the meantime the wicked are slumbering in appalling darkness and, filled with their sins, are going down into punishment. It does not seem the least surprising that a mortal man should be seized with such love for God, because in his secret heart he feels no other consolation than that which heaven gives. Like the notes of an organ he rises up to achieve his high and manifest desire, to contemplate God. What others intend to his hurt, he turns to glory, so that his soul already seems quite impervious to suffering: not even the fear of death can disturb him, nor anything whatever shake him out of his poise. For now he is moved by pressing love, and because his mind is constantly on Jesus he quickly discerns his own weaknesses, corrects them, and avoids them. So he consistently practises righteousness until such time as he is led up to his God, to sit with the heaven-born on an everlasting throne. This is the reason why he stands with a clear conscience, unwavering, unaffected by worldly depression, and never carried away by vainglory.

But those who persistently practise uncleanness cannot know any love for Christ, for what fires them is carnal lust. They cannot display the devotion which is God's due: they are firmly earthbound by the very weight of their desires. Consequently they are not destined to enjoy the delights of Paradise, for they persist in their perverse ways till they die. Quite rightly there is no mitigation of their grief, nor any alleviation of the pain of damnation: of their own free will they made sensual pleasure their good, and for a love that deceived they wantonly lost the love of their eternal Lover. So in everlasting punishment they will assuredly repent of their ever having sinned; yet they will never be purged by such suffering, but will burn in everlasting fire with none to comfort them.

CHAPTER 5

Why one must heed divine love rather than knowledge or argument.

O U T of all the various things that clamour for our attention, let us make it our prime concern to love God rather than to acquire knowledge or to engage in dialogue. For it is love that delights the soul and sweetens the conscience, because it draws it away from lesser pleasures and from the pursuit of one's own glory. *Knowledge without love does not edify*[1] or contribute to our eternal salvation; it merely *puffs up* to our own dreadful loss. So our spirit must be strong to undertake hard tasks for God's sake, its wisdom spiced with heaven, not the world. It must long to be enlightened with the wisdom of eternity, and glow with that lovely heat which urges us to long for and love the Maker himself; a heat which empowers us to spurn with our whole being everything merely transient. With regard to such things let a man consider it his greatest consolation that they do not endure, whereas he is one who has no present dwelling-place, but is always *seeking one to come, not built with hands.*[2] So he cries, *To me to live is Christ, and to die is gain.*[3]

Surely the man who refuses to yield to base pleasure is the man who loves God. A man's distance from the love of

1. 1 Corinthians 8 : 1.
2. cf. Hebrews 11 : 10, 16.
3. Philippians 1 : 21.

Christ is proportionate to his love of the world. If you really
love God your actions will show it, because by definition one
can never love him, and at the same time toy with evil
desires. Therefore I am quite prepared to say to all my
fellow exiles, 'Those who have never loved the Founder of
the universe will be cast into unending darkness. The experience of the everlasting heat of hell-fire is reserved for
those who do not want to love their Redeemer. What is
more, they will be excluded from the company of those who
praise the love of their Maker. Great their lament to find
themselves expelled from those who know Jesus to be their
joy and their jubilation! No splendour or coronation glory
for these! They deliberately chose to linger in worldly
luxury rather than to endure the penance and hardship
which would purge their sins, and bring them, now completely righteous, into the presence of the Foundation of all
good. But in this vale of tears (indeed, it is not so much a
place of joy as of toil!) their joy was to tread the broad and
slippery way; so now they languish in torments unbroken.'

For sinners cannot but grieve when they see the poor
borne up to unending peace, there to enjoy and to delight
in God the life-giver, there to behold the face of Christ.
Made beautiful through their virtues, these have blossomed
into happy and spiritual fervour; yet they never knew
much comfort in this world, nor shared in the pride of
those intoxicated with their own wisdom! Rather the reverse; they have had to endure the opposition of the
wicked, but every temptation has been overcome. Now they
are safe beside the throne of the Trinity, at peace. The
poison in their system has been truly eliminated, so now
they praise the life of the spirit both sincerely and gladly.
Their youthful antics and worldly folly they admit to merit
stern rebuke. Their thoughts are ever rising in loving song
to their Maker.

Therefore all those who are filled with love and joy, the
seekers after inextinguishable heat, unite to sing in one
glorious choir of rich melody; and now this company of
friends has the shade of heaven to protect them against the

scorching of lustful flattery and ill will. The very fervour of their sweet love ravishes them with the sight of their Beloved. Flowering through this loving flame into all virtue they rejoice in their Maker. Their mind is changed and passes into lasting melody. From now on their meditations become song. Melancholy has been driven out of the mansion of their spirit, and it now resounds with wondrous melody. The onetime torment of their soul has vanished, and now in glowing health they dwell in the heights of harmony, in the wonderful rhythm of sweet and melodious meditation.

When the time comes for them to leave this irksome, sick world, without a shadow of doubt they are borne up to God. Grief is no more, and there they sit among the seraphim. And it is all because they were completely absorbed in supreme love, an indescribable love that blazed in their souls, and made them love God with such sweetness and devotion. Fundamentally they knew nothing within themselves but spiritual heat, heavenly song, divine sweetness.

It follows that such people die without regret, and thereafter rise with joyful steps to the highest stage of eternal glory, their life crowned with the open vision of their Maker. Their song is absorbed into the most splendid praise, and their longing for him who rules all things is even more intense. And since they now behold openly the Face of Truth and are saturated with the sweetness of deity, it will occasion no surprise if they experience still greater wonders. When the bodies of the saints, now for a while held in the grasp of the earth, are raised from their graves and join up with their souls for the Last Judgement, they will stand out among the people, and will judge those to be condemned, and will make clear that even those who were only averagely good have been blessed by following after blessedness. And when the General Judgement is done they will be borne away to everlasting praise, and ascend with Christ to the utmost glory, and enjoy the vision of God for ever. From which we gather that everlasting sweetness completely fills their minds, and binds them now and hereafter with the indissoluble claim of love.

So it behoves us to make sure that the love of Christ is in us, and burning. This, rather than that we should indulge in futile discussion! For it is when our minds are giving way to unbridled curiosity that we lose the sweetness and delight of heaven. Nowadays too many are consumed with a desire for knowledge rather than for love, so that they scarcely know what love is or what is its delight. Yet all their study should have been directed to this end, so that they might be consumed with the love of God as well. Shame on them! An old woman can be more expert in the love of God – and less worldly too – than your theologian with his useless studying. He does it for vanity, to get a reputation, to obtain stipends and official positions. Such a fellow ought to be entitled not 'Doctor' but 'Fool'!

CHAPTER 6

About heretics, and faith in the Trinity.

TRUTH in plenty, whole and holy, reveals itself to those who look for it: 'closed books' are open to the sons of God. Then where does the treachery of the heretic spring from if not from his undisciplined and chaotic mind, blinded by its desire for its own reputation? For heretics never cease opposing God in their hearts by their insensate greed. Moreover when the Christian religion would cut away what is opposed to it, and make all agree in the unity of faith and love, they will openly resist truth by manifold argument. It is ever the way of the heretical and proud to ventilate new ideas and to question whatever the Church has asserted. Things that the faithful Christian holds dear they take pleasure in decrying.

We reject their errors, and assert the Son of God to be coeternal with the Father; this we must always believe and understand, for unless the Father had begotten him from all eternity, essentially he would not have been wholly God. For if there had been a time when God the Father had had

no Son, we would not be overstating the case if we said that
at such time God was less than he became afterwards when
he had begotten him! And that no right thinking man can
admit. The unchanging God begets unchanging God, and
has begotten him from eternity: nor does he cease to beget
him today. For neither can the substance of the Only Begotten sometimes be described as 'begotten', nor can the
substance of the Begetter ever be known apart from the Only
Begotten born of himself. Indeed the beginning of Deity
cannot be discovered either by reason or intellect – because
there was no beginning! Similarly the Son's Begetter abides
unchangeably in his eternal deity. In fact when in infinity
the wonder and the splendour of God Almighty shines out
clearly, whatever is human silliness aspiring to when it
asserts it knows the mystery inaudible to mortal ears? He
knows God perfectly who recognizes that he is beyond our
comprehension and capacity. For nothing can be known
perfectly if we do not know its origin and its purpose. In
this present life *we know in part and we understand in
part*,[1] but in the future life we shall know perfectly and
completely, as much as created beings can, and profitably
may. But he who wants information about our everlasting
Maker beyond what is useful undoubtedly falls short of
perfect understanding like a silly fool. You ask, 'What is
God?' and I answer briefly, 'He is such that no greater or
better exists or can exist.' If you are wanting to know in the
strict sense of the words what God is, my reply is that you
will find no answer to your question. I do not know; the
angels are ignorant; the archangels have not heard! How is
it then that *you* would know what is basically unknowable
and incommunicable? God himself, almighty as he is, is
unable to teach you what he is. For if you knew what God is
you would be as wise as God, which is something quite
beyond you, a creature. Stay then where you are, and do
not bother about going higher, because if you are wanting to know what God is you are wanting to be as God –
and that is all wrong! Face the fact: only God can know

1. 1 Corinthians 13:12.

himself. It is not weakness on God's part that he is unable
to teach you what he is in himself, but is due to his incred-
ible glory, because he cannot possibly be other than he is. If
it were really possible for him to be fully known, he would
not be incomprehensible. It is enough for you to know *that*
God is; to want to know *what* he is will only hinder.

It is a praiseworthy thing to be perfectly acquainted with
God, that is, to recognize that he is incomprehensible; and
recognizing him thus, to love him; and loving him, to rejoice in him; and rejoicing, to rest in him; and in inner
quiet to arrive at eternal rest. Do not worry if I have said
that you should be perfectly acquainted with God, and yet
have said that you cannot know God. You may object that
the Psalmist says, *Continue your loving kindness unto them
that know you.*[2] But if you are not to err you must understand the words, 'unto them that know you' in this way:
they mean 'unto those who know that you are a God who is
to be loved, praised, adored, glorified; the sole Creator of
everything, above all, through all, and in all, blessed for
ever and ever. Amen.'

CHAPTER 7

*In matters of divinity we ought not to talk of three Lords or
three Natures, because we speak of three Persons; a man is
great or small according to his love.*

IF people were to say, mistakenly, that there were three
beings, because they speak of three Persons in the Trinity,
why should they not go on to call them three Gods, since
each is with God, is God, and has the nature of God? We
say the Father is God, the Son is God, the Holy Spirit is
God. In the same way, the Father has the nature of God,
and so has the Son, and so has the Holy Spirit. Yet we are
not speaking of three Gods or three natures, but of one
God who is three Persons and one nature, and this we be-

2. Psalms 36:10.

lieve wholeheartedly. The divine majesty of the three Persons is all one, full and perfect, and each in himself contains the whole Godhead; he is equal and identical as regards the nature of deity, and the distinction is that which quite properly accords with the name. Thus there are three Persons and one God, one nature, one substance, one deity. And although 'Person' suggests to us a separate being – and here there are three Persons – it is not to be understood that there are three different natures. And just as we call our God, 'Father, Son, and Holy Spirit', and say there is one nature, not three, so we will speak of the same supreme Trinity as being three Persons and not one.

The Father is so called because of himself he has begotten the Son; the Son because he is begotten of the Father; the Holy Spirit because he is the Spirit of both, Holy Father and Holy Son. The Father who is life in the Son gave him his own total being, so that the Father is as much in the Son as he is in himself. And the Son is not less in the Father than he is in himself. What the Father is he received of no one, but what the Son is in his eternal birth he holds from the Father alone. Moreover the Holy Spirit comes from both Father and Son, and eternally exists in them and with them; nor is he more in himself than he is in them. For he is equal and coeternal with them from whom he comes, with the same being, the same nature, the same glory. He is the third Person in the Trinity. The eternal Son of the Father was made man in time, being born of a virgin that he might redeem the human race from the power of the devil. He is our Lord Jesus Christ – and may he be as firmly fixed in our thought as once he was, for our sakes, fixed to the Cross.

There is nothing so sweet as loving Christ, and because this is so let us not inquire too closely into matters we earthlings cannot possibly understand. In the Father's home there will be clearer light if we bring our whole heart to the loving of God. We shall all be *taught of God*[1] and so will rejoice in wonderful harmony. We shall have no

1. John 6:45.

greater pleasure or sweeter happiness than to praise our Maker – and there will be no more grief or weariness for ever!

It is the one who loves much who is truly great, and it is he who loves little who is less, for our worth before God accords with the degree of love in our hearts. On the human level however it does not happen like this, for it is he who has riches and possessions who is most respected and revered. Of course men ought not to think in such a way, but always honour and respect those whom they consider foremost in knowledge.

The great ones of this earth have no need at all except for their bodies or their possessions. The saints have chosen much greater splendour! Indeed they will have power to close heaven to those who have injured them and who refuse to repent; and to open it to those who have given them honour in God, and have supported them while in this exile – provided that their misfortunes arose through their charity, and that they repudiated all vainglory. So they ought to strive by all means in their power to acquire love, to hold on to it, and to retain it. Then in the day of temptation they can stand up to their enemies like men. Thus proved they will receive the crown of life. For love makes men whole: it is only those who love wholly who are allowed to scale the heights of the contemplative life.

Maybe the poor do live in squalor and dirt, but that is no reason to despise them; they are God's friends, Christ's brethren, when they bear the burden of their poverty with thankfulness. Those whom outwardly you might regard with contempt, inwardly you can honour as citizens of heaven. And just as you are developing your respect for them for God's sake, so he in his divine majesty continues his secret work, for he comforts them as he says *Blessed are the poor, for yours is the Kingdom of God.*[2] The great suffering and poverty they experience in this life means the purging of their sins, for when a poor man is being afflicted in body by hunger and thirst, by cold and nakedness, and

2. Luke 6:20.

by all the other trials of this world, in soul he is being cleansed from earthly filth and dirt. The poor, to be sure, will not find their future and eternal rest any less sweet for having had to put up with their present hardship. It will be said of them, *We have been glad of the days in which you have plagued us, and for the years in which we have seen evil.*[3] So welcome joyfully the bearing of poverty, and set your mind to endure cheerfully all the other trials. Patience in tribulation will make you worthy to attain eternal peace and glory.

CHAPTER 8

A perfect lover of God would rather incur great punishment than offend God by a single sin; why God afflicts the righteous with the ungodly.

OUT of this vast fire of love such beauty and virtue is developed in the soul that the righteous man would choose to face the utmost punishment rather than for one moment offend God – though he would also know that by penitence he might rise again, and subsequently be more pleasing to God, and more holy too. Because the perfect man, whoever he is, knows this: nothing is dearer to God than innocence, nothing more pleasing than good will. And if we are really to love God, we ought to be willing to lose the great reward of heaven rather than to commit a single sin however venial. Supreme righteousness asks no reward for being righteous, but only for the friendship of God, and that because he is what he is. It is always better to endure hardship, than even for a moment to be consciously and deliberately enticed away from righteousness.

It is clear that those who love Christ with such fervour as never to want to sin again, not only will be free from punishment, but will rejoice for ever with the angel hosts.

3. Psalms 90: 15.

Chapter 8

But those who give themselves up to evil doing, who depend on filth and carnal pleasure for their enjoyment – they consider them important and desirable, and pretend they are essential – in one fell swoop will both lose the good (*sic*) they love, and gain the evil they did not bargain for!

But almost certainly someone is going to ask why does God Almighty chastise the righteous and the ungodly alike? You will have noticed that when men are threshing, they flail chaff as well as grain. When they are winnowing they throw the chaff out, but the grain is carefully collected for human consumption. If we were all to live good lives, no doubt we should all live in peace and quiet without discord or war. But because evil folk are many, and the good are few, many evil things result; and evil has to be punished. Evil things happen to good men of course because they are involved with evil till they die. The righteous, in order to prevent this sinful tendency coming to a head, are 'instructed' by the rod of their loving Father to accept their present easy discipline, and thereby escape future tribulation. So if you yourself are going through persecution or wretchedness or misery, you are experiencing what is exactly right for your present circumstances. For are you not in fact in a 'vale of tribulation'? How can you then be wanting to rejoice in what after all is a prison, to flourish greatly in what is our exile, to travel trouble-free throughout the whole length of our journey? Let us remember that Christ and his apostles suffered, and you are wanting to go from one joy to another. It just cannot be done! For either the fire of divine love will burn up the canker of our sins in this life here, purifying our souls to be fit to fly up to God, or after this life the flames of purgatory will torment these same souls. If they are to escape hell, or if, indeed, there is not love strong enough to burn us up wholly, it will be essential for us to be cleansed by tribulation, sickness, and grief.

Further, we know this – and there is no doubt about it – that no young man who is surrounded by feminine beauty and flattery and sweet nothings and enervating luxury can possibly be holy, unless it is through grace, great and exceptional. So many and such like things are asking for trouble, and all too often bring a holy man down. I reckon it a major miracle when a man through God's grace and a love for Christ spurns these allurements completely, and out of the midst of them all (which war against his soul, however pleasant they be to his flesh), rises like a man to the utmost heights of heavenly contemplation. There is no doubt that he is more holy as a result of all this, and inwardly much richer through the comfort brought him by his love of God. If he was thrown into the fire of hell he would not burn! For he has completely extinguished the seductions and delights of life which come to him from outside. It is not surprising, even if it is unusual, that Christ works thus in some of his beloved. It is said of such *He has spread a cloud*[1] (obviously a 'cloud of divine grace) *for a covering* (from carnal lust, by the fire of everlasting love) *and fire to give light* (within their mind) *in the night* (of this life); and all this lest they should be taken captive by the attraction of empty beauty. But Christ's love burns in them with such sweetness that they deem every carnal, illicit pleasure the most appalling filth, and trample it down.

Therefore you are not to touch these slippery things which are unlawful for you either to want or to have. Remember that you are to discipline your hands, your tongue, your appetite, and not be enticed by women. Maybe incitement to soft living is wrapped up with being a man or a woman – and hot food and drink by their very warmth inflame the flesh unduly! Men are ever fashioning comfort for their bodies, and destruction for their souls. These must be eschewed by the chaste.

1. Psalms 105:39.

CHAPTER 9

*In adversity God is to be praised and loved; good men are
pleasant and humble.*

I F temporal honour can be destroyed by shame, and
earthly glory finished by confusion, it seems to be un-
doubted that an insult is better than honour, confusion
than success, grief than glory. It is by these latter things
that a man often enough lapses into vainglory. Yet if he
habitually faced the former with patience he would learn
humility in this life here, and escape punishment in the life
to come, because God does not punish the just twice. More,
he would be crowned in splendour because the patience of
the poor will not ultimately perish.

These are the things that belong to holiness: first, never
to think, say, or do what displeases God and, then, to think,
say, and do what does please him! Do this as well as you
know how, so as not to cause offence, and do not pretend to
a holiness that is not yours. A man is a fool if he is always
wanting to appear holy, just as a good man would be abnor-
mal if he wanted to seem bad. There are some things which
looked at by themselves are neither good nor bad; which in
their natural state are worth neither praise nor blame. The
doing of such things does not displease God any more than
does their omission. We can see, hear, smell, feel or touch
them, and be no better off – or worse either. All sin, however,
shows a contempt of God, or is done to hurt one's neighbour, or to harm oneself. But many human matters are
none of these things. All the same, to be despised or to be
made a fool of in front of others helps a man rise to the joy
of the angels!

Good Jesus, scourge me, wound me, slay me, burn me;
   do with me here and now whatever in your goodness
      you decide;

that in the days to come I may know and feel
  not evil but your love – and that, for ever!

To be despised, rejected, insulted by all,
    for your sake, is sweeter to me
than to be called the brother of any earthly monarch,
    honoured among men, and praised by all.

In this present life I would know misery as my lot in
      every place,
  if I might be spared by you, my God, these things in
    the other!
It is here I would suffer, and be put right;
  Christ grant me this now in the present,
    if I may not otherwise escape punishment in the
      future!

But the conceited and touchy consider themselves so
magnificent as to be beyond any possibility of suffering. Yet
the least word can often upset them, and for no reason at
all. It is better to avoid them rather than argue with them,
because they never let go. They defend whatever position
they take up, however false or wrong it may be. They cannot be persuaded by reason or authority because they are
not going to be seen to be beaten or ridiculous. Even when
they are ignorant (and know it) they still would be
thought inspired in everything that has to do with God, so
as to lay the law down everywhere without fear of contra-
diction. They would even prefer to remain in error than that
they should be publicly accused of it!

My brothers, give up this mad pride, and proud madness!
Let us be genuinely humble all through life. It is better, and
a good and lovely thing, to have Christ tell us, after we
have died, *Friend, go up higher,*[1] rather than that he
should say, *Fool, go down lower.* For this is what will
happen to the lowly and the lofty. A righteous man need
not fear tribulation, grief, misery, perplexity, or rejection:
at least, all the while he does not sin, and is advancing in

1. Luke 14:10.

contemplation and love for God. For before we can arrive at the court of the King where with the angels and saints of God we shall rejoice in sweet plenty, we must ourselves be proved here below, whether it is by flattery or detraction, by blandishment or backbiting, by praise or calumny. In patient humility and love we must cleave to the precepts and counsels of Christ so that when judgement is given it can be said of us, even as it has been written, *As gold in the furnace is tried, so he proved them.*[2] On every side there has been fire, and *he found them worthy of himself.*[3] In this way we pass through things pleasant and unpleasant, through fire and water, until we attain the living rest of heaven. So in every unpleasant situation, be it hardship or poverty, remember never to murmur or speak foolishly or perversely. If *in everything you give thanks,*[4] with all the more joy will you be raised to the kingdom of the saints – always assuming that you have voluntarily endured in the world those things of which we have been speaking.

My soul, whatever happens, praise the Lord with delight and devotion. With your praise, taste its sweetness; with your song, its honey. *While I live I will praise the Lord.*[5] Whether I suffer or prosper, face insult or honour, *I will praise my God while I have my being.*[6] If I rest in Jesus I will rejoice: if I undergo persecution I will not forget the love of God. I only ask to love God and to attain him. I can do nothing else; my one concern is to love Christ. So far I have not reached the love of God as did my predecessors; and they did many useful things beside. Wherefore I hang my head and *shame has covered my face.*[7] So, Lord, make my heart bigger, better able to perceive your love. For the greater a man's capacity, the fuller the love he gets and savours, and the less his concern for the flesh. But even this must be with common sense, so that it may accord with the saying of the wise man, *I travailed but little, and I found much rest.*[8] For after the few years of life here, the right-

2. Wisdom 3:6. 3. Wisdom 3:5.
4. 1 Thessalonians 5:18. 5, 6. Psalms 104:33.
7. Jeremiah 51:51. 8. Ecclesiasticus 51:27.

eous man finds rest for eternity. For while God's saint and lover is in exile here he reveals himself to be a man neither too lighthearted nor too sad. There is a maturity about his cheerfulness.

There are some who disapprove of laughter, and others who praise it. The laughter of a frivolous, silly mind can be reprehensible, but surely that which springs from a cheerful conscience and spiritual buoyancy is worth praising? Only the righteous have it, and they call it *delighting in the love of God*. Yet when we are cheerful and joyful the irreligious call us 'dissolute'; and when we are serious they call us 'hypocrites'! It is unusual for a man to assess as good in another what he does not find in himself, and the sins at which he stumbles he attributes to other folk too. It is the act of a presumptuous man to think that if others do not follow his own particular way of life they are depraved and deceived! And the cause of it all? He has let go humility.

The stages of humility are these: to keep one's eyes down rather than up; to be restrained in speech, and not exaggerated; to listen gladly to those who are better and wiser than oneself; to want others' wisdom to be heard rather than one's own; not to speak out of turn; not to run away from everyday life; to prefer others to oneself; to recognize one's weaknesses; and to reckon oneself the least of all. Were I really anxious to mix with people my ambition would be to sit in the lowest place, with my reputation minimal, so that I might glory in Christ Jesus, caring nothing for human praise or blame, but eager to be united in devotion to God.

For many of those who used to speak with me were like scorpions: with their head they oozed flattery, and with their tail they struck slanders. From whose lying lips and deceitful tongues may God deliver my soul, and establish it in peace and joy!

But where does such madness in the minds of men come from? No one likes to be belittled; no one likes to be reproved; everyone wants to be praised. People rejoice in honours, and are delighted by applause – and this is true of some who have a reputation for sanctity of life. Such people seem to me either too holy for words, or else complete fools, though men call them wise and learned. For what sane man is going to abandon himself to dissipation, and enjoy the empty words of men? If he has a good look at himself, and takes the trouble to learn what sort of man he is in thought and deed, he will find out soon enough, and discover whether he is deserving of praise or blame. And when he sees that in many things he is blameworthy, and laudable only in few, he is not going light-heartedly to accept the honour and favour which he does not deserve – not unless he is mentally deranged. But if in his self-investigation he finds he is glowing with the heat and sweetness of divine love beyond description, and he is setting out on the contemplative life, and is committed thereto, and if moreover he cannot recall ever having committed grave sins or, having committed them, believes them to have been wiped out by penance, he is certainly not going to grieve that men do not honour him; his reward is much greater: his fellowship is with the angels! The man of such disposition takes no more pleasure in sitting next to a king than to a pauper, because he is considering, not the riches and dignities of men generally, but the life and merits of each one singly. He does not regard it as important that he should glitter with gold or be attended by a huge retinue, or go about in episcopal purple, or wear a mitre. No indeed: he esteems a holy and sweet conscience better than all these things and delights.

CHAPTER 10

The lover of God despises the world, weariness and idleness;
about hypocrites and covetous men.

I⊤ is said in the Canticles that *love is strong as death,*
jealousy is as cruel as hell.[1] Death does indeed slay the living,
and hell does not spare the dead. So too, when the love of
God takes complete charge of a man, not only does it kill the
root of his love for the world, but since he is now dead to
the world and one with heaven it fires him to bear for God's
sake whatever tribulation and misery life may bring. You
who reckon you love Christ pay attention to this: if you
still regard earthly things with pleasure your soul will be
unprepared to endure suffering or death. And you will show
clearly that you are not a true lover of God. Indeed a true
lover of God never lets his eye linger on the world, and if it
is for God's sake, nor does he fear suffering. He allows
nothing to take his mind off the Beloved.

And you, a lover of God (or at least desperately anxious
to be one!) must study always as best you know how, and
with the help of Christ's grace, not to be ensnared by boredom or affected by sloth. And should your prized facility of
prayer or meditation desert you and you cannot raise your
mind to joyful and holy contemplation or sing as once you
did, you are not on that account to give up your reading or
praying or whatever other useful thing you do, be it outward or inward, lest you degenerate into sloth. Boredom
drags many people down into sloth, and sloth into carelessness and sin. Therefore you must always be as fervent as
you can, and not let your affections go after any worldly
thing you covet. No one can be united to God perfectly
while he is held by a liking for the created and worldly.

There are some indeed who seem outwardly united to
God, who inwardly are given over to the devil: impostors

1. Canticles (or Song or Songs) 8:6.

74

who ostensibly despise the world, but who in fact love it!
They wish to appear to speak of God, though their hearts
are so possessed with the love of money that sometimes
they will fall out over a farthing! They serve God with
their lips, but are wholly devoid of devotion. And though
they have no real faith or love they seem by the way they
behave and dress and speak to be the most holy of men.
Moreover, people like these profess themselves to be steadfast in light affliction, but when they come up against what
must be firmly resisted, then they at once break and fall
down. And what was once hidden is now wide open for all
to see! When they are rolling in money or living on the fat
of the land they protest that they are eating next to
nothing: it is their conviction that the whole world is no
more than vanity, and therefore (they claim) they can
barely survive because of their weakness.

They are deceivers: theirs is the wisdom of the world.
They deceive in this way so as not to be seen in their other
ploys, inasmuch as they are on guard against worldly loss,
disguising their real contempt for eternal things under a
specious greed for 'spiritual quiet'. But however much they
may conceal for a while, there can be no doubt that long
before the end, or at all events *at* the end, they will be
recognized for what they are. When they give alms, or do
any other good deed, they do it publicly, so that everything
shall be seen by men.[2] They deservedly provoke the wrath
of God because they do not really want to be perfect but
only to seem so. In their heart, which is where God sees
them, true humility is lacking, and they are after their own
glory, and not God's. It is extremely difficult to have riches
and not to love them, and it is no less difficult to hold a
profitable job or position and not to want more.

Whence it happens that often among people priests are
denigrated: if they are chaste they are found to be avari-
cious; if they are generous they are dissolute. Often enough it
happens that those who have taken priest's Orders fall more
deeply into sin, the more so because they have taken this

2. Matthew 6:1.

step unworthily. Some, in truth, carried away by worry or greed, plead future infirmity or poverty, and say they are amassing goods against impending misery. But these are just a joke to the demons, because not only do they let the good things of life slip through their fingers, but the very calamities they fear they run into, since they leave no place for God, who delivers his servants in his sight. Worst of all, when they are full up inside with worldly coveting, outwardly they reckon to shine in the odour of sanctity. But the servant of God puts his trust in God, and such goods as he has beyond his immediate requirements he distributes to the needy. On the other hand the servant of the world seeks to keep everything for himself, for he is insatiably greedy and evil. Moreover, he is so miserly that he can only bring himself to eat what is cheap and nasty, since it is by being mean that he amasses much money. These are those whom the Psalmist condemns, *His enemies shall lick the dust.*[3]

CHAPTER 11

The lovers of God will judge with him; the love of knowledge that has been acquired, and the love of God; the true lover of God does not err, nor is he deceivd by fastings, abstinence, advice, or presumption.

SINCE the human soul is capable of receiving God alone, nothing less than God can fill it; which explains why lovers of earthly things are never satisfied. The peace known by lovers of Christ comes from their heart being fixed, in longing and in thought, in the love of God; it is a peace that sings and loves and burns and contemplates. Very sweet indeed is the quiet which the spirit experiences. Music, divine and delectable, comes to rejoice it; the mind is rapt in sublime and gay melody and sings the delights of everlasting love. Now from human lips sounds forth again the praise of God; the praise too, of the Blessed Virgin in

3. Psalms 72:9.

whom he glories beyond measure. This need occasion no surprise, for the heart of the singer is altogether ablaze with heavenly fire. And he is transformed into the likeness of him in whom is all melody and song, and is transported by loving desire for the taste of heaven. A man overflows with inner joy, and his very thought sings as he rejoices in the warmth of his love. All this, to be sure, is meaningless to those who are 'dead', and an outsider cannot understand how anything so sweet and lovely is experienced by a man in a decaying body, limited by its very mortality. But even the one who has all this himself wonders at it, and rejoices at the unspeakable goodness of God who *gives liberally and does not upbraid*,[1] for it is from him the experience comes. Moreover when he has once had experience of that great thing (and it is a great thing, completely unknown by dying men) he knows that when it is missing he is never at ease, but is always pining for love. So he remains vigilant, and sings and thinks of his love and his Beloved – and if he is on his own sings all the more blithely!

Once a man has known some such experience, he is never thereafter wholly without it, for there always remains a sort of glow, some song or sweetness, even if these are not all present together in equal strength. Yet all are present, unless illness catches him, or he is gripped by intolerable hunger or thirst, or is held up by cold, or heat, or travel. It behoves him then who would sing his love for God and rejoice fervently in such singing, to pass his days in solitude. Yet the abstinence in which he lives should not be excessive, nor on the other hand should he display too much extravagance. Better for him slightly to exceed the limit if it is done in ignorance and with the sound intention of sustaining the body, than that he should falter by over strict fasting, and through physical weakness be unable to sing. But, to be sure, he who is chosen for this life is not overcome by the devil's deceit whether he eats or abstains. The true lover of Christ, one who is taught by him, does not worry overmuch whether there is too much or too little.

1. James 1:5.

He will deserve infinitely more by his joyful song, by his prayer and contemplation, by his reading and meditation, yes, and by his discretion in eating, than if, without it, he were ever fasting, or only eating bread and vegetables while he prayed and read. I myself have eaten and drunk things that are considered delicacies; not because I love such dainties, but in order to sustain my being in the service of God, and in the joy of Christ. For his sake I conformed quite properly to those with whom I was living lest I should invent a sanctity where none existed; lest men should over-praise me where I was less worthy of praise.

On the other hand there are many from whom I have parted, not because they fed me ill or badly, but because our ways of life were not compatible, or for some other adequate reason. Yet I venture to say with blessed Job, *Fools did despise me, and when I parted from them they turned against me.*[2] Nevertheless those who said I was not willing to stay in any place where I was not comfortably fed will blush when they see me. It is better to see what I despise than to desire what I fail to see. Fasting is effective in the control of the desires of carnal lust, and in the mastery of a wild and wayward mind. But in him who attains the heights of contemplation with joy and ardent love, the desires of the flesh now lie virtually dead. It means death to evil longings for the man who surrenders himself to contemplation, whose inner self is being changed to a glory and pattern that is different. Now it is *no longer he who lives, but Christ who lives in him,*[3] and as a result he is overwhelmed by love and longing for him. He almost dies because it is so beautiful; he can hardly live because of such love.

> His is the soul that says,
> *tell my Beloved I am pining for love;*[4]
> I am wanting to die;
> I long to pass away;
> I am burning to pass over.

2. Job 19:18.   3. Galatians 2:20.   4. Canticles 5:8.

Chapter 11

> See I am dying through love!
> Come down, Lord.
> Come, Beloved, and ease my longing.
> See how I love, I sing, I glow, I burn.
> Spare a thought for this poor wretch:
>   order me to be brought before you.

He who has this joy here, and glories in it now, is inspired by the Holy Spirit. He cannot go wrong: he can do what he likes, and he will be safe. No mortal man can give him such sound advice as that which he has within himself from God Eternal. If others would advise him, they will surely go astray because they do not know what is happening. But he himself will not go wrong however much he might wish to agree with their advice, because God will not permit it; for God keeps him within his will, so that he does not go beyond it. Of such it is said, *The spiritual man judges all things, and himself is judged by no man.*[5]

No one ought to assume, however, that he is one such just because his renunciation of the world is perfect, and his entrance into the solitary state irreproachable, and his contemplation of things supernal transcendent. This grace is not given to all contemplatives, but only rarely and to very few, and then to those who attain to supreme quiet of mind and body; they are chosen solely for the business of loving God. It is difficult to find such men, who are few and far between; they are held very dear, and are much sought after, loved by God and man. Angels rejoice when they quit this life, for they are fit for angelic company. On the other hand, there are many who in great devotion and sweetness offer their prayers to God, and through their prayer and meditation are able to taste the delights of contemplation, who do not move on but remain in their quiet state.

5. 1 Corinthians 2:15.

CHAPTER 12

About not judging another, but rather giving thanks; the
eight results of loving God; about avoiding the company of
women.

THE man who lives a holy and righteous life is not going to
despise sinners, however bad. Those who are tempted fall
because they have not the grace to resist – though it was
through their own sinfulness that they turned from good to
evil. No one can do good, or love God, or be chaste, unless
God enables him to do so. So if you get puffed up because
you have done well, or have kept off carnal pleasures, or
have endured hard penance (and consequently have received the praise of human lips!) you should remember
that unless Christ in his kindness had protected you, you
would have fallen into similar evils as did the bad man – or
worse. You have no power to resist of your own, but only
his power of whom it is said, *I will love you, Lord, my
strength.*[1] If therefore you have nothing that in the first
place you did not receive, *why do you boast as if you had
not received it?*[2] I thank my God, who not for any merit of
mine but solely for my good and his own glory so chastised
me his child, and so frightened me his servant, that to me it
seemed sweet to flee from the 'delights' of the world (which
in any case are few and fleeting) and to escape the many,
never-ending pains of hell. Moreover this was the way he
taught me, and through that teaching endowed me with
such strength that I can now gladly put up with present,
difficult, penance, especially since I am to come so easily to
eternal delight and full reward. For if we want to, even in
this life and without undue hardship, we can repent completely and purge ourselves of our sins, so long as we destroy all those sins to the best of our ability. If in fact we
are not cleansed here, in time to come we shall find the

1. Psalms 18:1.　　　　　　2. 1 Corinthians 4:7.

Apostle speaks the truth when he says, *It is a fearful thing
to fall into the hands of the living God.*[3]

> Lord God, pity me: my infancy was stupid,
>   my boyhood vain, my adolescence unclean.
> But now, Lord Jesus, my heart has been set on fire with
>   holy love,
>   and my disposition has been changed,
>   so that my soul has no wish to touch those bitter things
>   which once were meat and drink to me.

Such are my affections now that it is nothing but sin I
hate, none but God I fear to offend, nothing but God in
which I rejoice. My only grief is for sin, my only love is
God, my only hope is in him. Nothing saddens me except
wrong, nothing pleases me except Christ.

Yet there was a time when I was rebuked, quite properly,
by three different women. One rebuked me because in my
eagerness to restrain the feminine craze for dressy and suggestive clothes I inspected too closely their extravagant
ornamentation. She said I ought not to notice them so as to
know whether they were wearing horned head-dresses or
not. I think she was right to reprove me. Another rebuked
me because I spoke of her great bosom as if it pleased me.
She said, 'What business is it of yours whether it is big or
little?' She too was right. The third jokingly took me up
when I appeared to be going to touch her somewhat rudely,
and perhaps had already done so, by saying, 'Calm down,
brother!' It was as if she had said, 'It doesn't go with your
office of hermit to be fooling with women.' She too deservedly made me feel uncomfortable. I ought to have held
off rather than to have behaved this way. When I came to
myself[4] I thanked God for teaching me what was right
through their words, and for showing me a more pleasant
way than my previous one, so that I might cooperate more
fully with Christ's grace. I am not going to put myself in
the wrong with women henceforward.

3. Hebrews 10:31.   4. cf. Luke 15:17.

A fourth woman with whom I was in some way familiar did not so much rebuke me as despise me when she said 'You are no more than a beautiful face and a lovely voice: you have *done* nothing.' I think it better therefore to dispense with whatever their particular contribution to life is, rather than to fall into their hands, hands which know no moderation whether loving or despising! Yet these things happened because I was seeking their salvation, and not because I was after anything improper. What is more, they were the very people from whom I had for a while received physical sustenance!

CHAPTER 13

The solitary life, and the hermit's, is superior to the communal or mixed life; how it leads to the fire of love, and to joyful sweetness.

THERE have been people, and there probably still are, who have without hesitation put communal life above the solitary. They urge us to hurry towards life in community if we want to attain the heights of perfection. It is not necessary to say much by way of argument against such folk, since the only life they approve of is the one they want to practise, or at least know something about. In other words they do not approve of the solitary life because they know nothing about it. It is a life which no one who 'lives in the flesh' can know, but only he to whom it has been given by God. No one can assess it rightly who is uncertain about it and the way it works. I do not doubt that if they did in fact have some knowledge of the life, it would be this life they would be praising rather than the other.

But a worse mistake is to keep on denigrating the solitary life, and to abuse it. They cry, 'Woe to him who is alone!' They do not define 'alone' as being 'without God', but understand it to mean 'without company'. A man is alone indeed if God is not with him. For when he dies he is taken at once for punishment, and is for ever cut off from the vision of the glory of God and his saints. On the other hand he who for God's sake has chosen the solitary life, and lives it properly, knows not so much 'woe' as 'wonderful strength', and rejoices continually as he recalls the Name of Jesus. The less men fear to embrace for God a life that has no human comfort, the more will it be given them to glory in divine consolation. For they are the recipients of frequent spiritual visitations which certainly they would not know in community. It is for this reason the beloved soul is told, *I will lead her into solitude, and I will speak to her heart.*[1] There are those who have been divinely taught to seek solitude for Christ's sake, and to hold on to it tight. And at once, in order to serve God with greater freedom and devotion, they have relinquished the habit of the community. They have spurned and rejected the transitory, and in the sublimity of their mind have risen above the temporal. Their sole desire is for the joys which are eternal; and so they make time for devotion and contemplation, never wavering in their wholehearted effort to love Christ. Many of their number, although they live physically among people, are mentally remote from them; they never falter in their heavenly longing, because in spirit they are far removed from a sinful way of life.

Thus hermits rightly have one controlling motive: they live loving God and their neighbour; they despise worldly approval; they flee, so far as they may, from the face of man; they hold all men more worthy than themselves; they give their minds continually to devotion; they hate idleness; they withstand manfully the pleasures of the flesh; they taste and seek ardently heavenly things; they leave earthly things on one side without coveting them; and they find their delight in the sweetness of prayer.

Some of them, indeed, genuinely experience the sweetness of heavenly refreshment. Chaste in heart and body, with mental vision unsullied, they behold the citizens of heaven, and look on God himself. Because here they have loved the

1. Hosea 2:14

bitter cup of penance and hard toil, there they are consumed with unending and loving contemplation; they are fit to wait on God, and to await the kingdom of Christ.

A hermit's life is a great one if it is greatly lived! Take for instance, the blessed Maglorious, a miraculous man if ever there was one, and who had rejoiced in angelic visits from childhood. As his predecessor, the blessed Sampson, had foretold, he was made an archbishop, and he ruled the Church of God both long and laudably. But an angel visited him with heavenly counsel, with the result that he gave up his archbishopric, and chose to live as a hermit. And at the end of his life his passing was revealed to him. Similarly the blessed Cuthbert exchanged the life of a bishop for that of an anchorite.[2]

If then men of this quality have done such things to deserve greater reward what man in his senses would dare to set another state of life in the church above the solitary? In this state men are occupied with nothing outward, but give themselves totally to divine contemplation, so as to be on fire with love for Christ, the cares of the world put behind

2. Of these three saints the only one about which there is much factual information is St Cuthbert. But hagiographers have not been slow to fill the gaps with improving legends, which when they are not improbable can be quite fantastic. It seems that St Sampson (*c.* 490–565) was a Welshman, who in the course of his episcopate migrated from Cornwall to Brittany, where he founded a monastery at Dol. His evangelistic efforts spread beyond the French mainland, for his name is associated with the Channel Islands of Jersey and Guernsey. He had a great name for miracles. His cousin, St Maglorious, was a monk in his monastery. When Sampson died Maglorious succeeded him in the bishopric, a post which he later relinquished in order to retire to Sark. There he founded his own monastery, becoming its first abbot. Angels clearly played a large part in his thinking, for his traditional emblem shows him giving one of them Holy Communion. He died *c.* 586. Perhaps the greatest of these three was the Northumbrian, St Cuthbert, who after a life of devoted pastoral and evangelistic work resigned the see of Hexham to live as a solitary on Farne. He died there in 684. The *Penguin Dictionary of Saints* describes him as 'a man of extraordinary charm and practical ability, who attracted people deeply by the beauty of holiness'. Durham Cathedral is still his shrine.

them. And so celestial music resounds amongst them, and
sweet flowing melody rejoices the solitary. From such
melody the man who lives in the midst of clatter is distracted, and can but rarely meditate or pray.

It is of the solitary that the Psalmist speaks when he tells
of the lover's hymns, *I will go into the place of his wonderful tabernacle, up to the house of God.*[3] The way he goes,
rejoicing and praising, is thus described, *In the voice of
praise and thanksgiving, the sound of the banquet.*[4] And to
show that solitude is essential for this, so that away from
physical racket and song man may capture and retain some
of the joy of that sound, he demonstrates elsewhere quite
clearly, *I would get me away far off, and remain in solitude.*[5]

For in this life he is straining every nerve to burn with
the fire of the Holy Spirit and, captured as well as consoled
by the delight of love, to exult in God. So the perfect solitary will burn vigorously in his love for God, and when he
is 'above himself', in ecstasy through contemplation, he is
lifted up to celestial joy and song and sound. Such a man
indeed is like the seraphim: there is an inner blaze of indescribable and unwavering charity. His heart is shaped by
the divine fire and, ablaze beyond description, he is borne to
his Beloved. Indeed, at death he is taken up at once to the
chiefest seats of heaven, that he may dwell serenely, in
place of Lucifer. This will be his lot because he has been
fired with indescribable love, and has sought the glory of
his Creator alone, and yet has walked humbly, and has not
thought himself better than the rest of sinful men.

3. cf. Psalms 43:3.
4. cf. Psalms 42:5 (B.C.P.).
5. Psalms 55:7.

CHAPTER 14

Praise for the solitary life, and its first lovers; the love of God consists in warmth, song, and sweetness; quiet is necessary for it; such men are saved from delusions, and are not preferred to ecclesiastical office.

THE blessed Job who was taught the hard way by the Holy Spirit sums up in a word the multifarious reasons for approving saintly hermits in the passage, *Who set the wild ass free.*[1]

In the first place, the freedom of grace is commended in the saying *Who set the wild ass free.* Secondly, there is reference to the rejection of carnal affection in the words, *and he loosed their chains.* Thirdly, there is the solitary life itself in *he gave them a house in the wilderness.* And in the fourth place, the longing for everlasting bliss is in the saying *his tent is in the salty earth.* Salt does not quench thirst, but rather aggravates it. Those who perceive something of the sweetness of eternal life desire all the more fervently to get hold of it, and sample it.

Indeed, Saint John Baptist, the prince of hermits (our Lord excepted) was not behind in his affection, for he chose the solitary life. Others in like manner have chosen it – the locust, for example, who according to Solomon has *neither* prince, *King*, nor master, *yet go they forth by bands*[2] of virtue and gifts!

Now there are two sorts of chains: those of nature and sin, which in the case of solitaries God has broken asunder, and those of love, which he has strengthened. The *house in the wilderness* can also refer to 'quietness of heart', because holy hermits, away from tumult and town, experience

1. The passage in Job 39:5–6 runs thus: 'Who hath sent out the wild ass free? or who hath loosed the bands of the wild ass? Whose house I have made the wilderness, and the barren land his dwellings.' Rolle is quoting from the Vulgate version.
2. Proverbs 30:27.

sweetness with a clear conscience through the generosity of Christ. They rejoice to sing of everlasting love; they refresh themselves, and relax in delightful warmth. And though in the body they suffer hardship and adversity, yet in the spirit they maintain a constant harmony and fervour.

But there is an evil solitude, a solitude of pride, which occurs when one sets himself up above the rest, or ascribes his gifts to his own strength of will. It is to these that the saying applies, *Woe to him who is alone when he falls; for he has not another to help him up.*[3] Admittedly in the beginning of their new life (I am not speaking of the *girovagi*[4] who are an eremitic scandal!) hermits inevitably are wearied by many different temptations. But after the storm of evil promptings God infuses them with the calm of holy desires. And if they exercise these desires vigorously with tears and meditation and prayer, seeking only to love Christ, they will soon make them feel that they are now living more in pleasure than in grief, worry, or toil. They will have him whom they have loved, sought, and longed for. Then indeed they will rejoice and not grieve! For what is rejoicing if it is not the attaining of the good one has longed for, the brooding on it, the relaxing in it? Small wonder if there is cheer when true lovers meet, and mutual joy in their physical contact. It is quite impossible to describe the ardent longing of those in love. The exchange of sight and speech is sweeter to them than honey and the honeycomb!

Jeremiah, too, commends the solitary life. *It is good for a man to bear the yoke of the Lord in his youth. He will sit in solitude and quiet, and will raise himself up*[5] because he longs for and contemplates eternal things. So it is that in Ecclesiasticus we read, *On earth the man has not been born who is like Enoch*[6] for he was *caught up from the earth.*

3. Ecclesiastes 4: 10.
4. Tramplike solitaries who cadged their way from place to place. They are invariably condemned in Christian literature, yet their numbers persisted.
5. Lamentations 3: 27.   6. Ecclesiasticus 49: 14.

For contemplatives are superior to other men, both in the outstanding quality of their work, and in the fervour of their love.

All the while he is indifferent to worldly power love indwells the heart of the solitary. Herein is the foundation of his fervour and his longing for light, because he is tasting the things of heaven and singing his honeyed (not heavy!) song. He offers his praise to his noble Lover, like the seraphim, and since his loving mind is in tune with theirs he says, 'See how I burn in my love; how hungrily I long!' So is the lover's soul consumed with indescribable fire, shot through with that flame which gladdens and glitters with heavenly light. There is no end that I can discover to this fervour and happiness, and as I am always pressing on towards the object of my love it means that death becomes sweet to me as well as sure.

Because for the sake of the Saviour the holy hermit has made solitude his home, in heaven he will receive a dwelling, golden and glistening, and in the midst of the angelic orders. Because for love of his Creator he dressed in filthy rags, his Maker will clothe him in eternal splendour. Because once he was prepared to live here with features wan and drawn, so now his countenance shines with wonderful glory. In exchange for his revolting garments he will wear raiment glorious and resplendent with precious stones, for ever in the midst of those who dwell in Paradise. Because he has purged himself from vices and avoided all ostentation and has done with all appearance of filth, his warm love for Almighty God has gained for him a song which is sweet and heavenly. The harmonies of those who praise divine charity have filled his mind, and rightly so. And thus it is with courage and not dread that he quits his exile here; and at the end of all he hears angelic song, and rises up, he who has loved so ardently; he is caught up to that eternal hall, and honoured in the most splendid fashion, to sit on high with the seraphim.

As far as my study of Scripture goes, I have found that to love Christ above all else will involve three things: warmth and song and sweetness. And these three, as I know from personal experience, cannot exist for long without there being great quiet.

If I were to stand up when I was engaged in contemplation or to walk about or even to lie prostrate on the ground I found that I failed to attain these three, and even seemed to be left in dryness. Consequently, if I were to hold on to and retain deep devotion I must sit – which is what I have decided to do. I am aware that there is an underlying reason for this, for if a man does much standing and walking his body gets tired, and thus his soul too is hindered, wearied, and burdened. He is not as quiet as he can be and so is not in his most perfect state; if the philosopher[7] is right, it is the quiet sitting that makes the soul wise. Let him who still stands more than he sits when delighting in the things of God recognize he has a long way to go before he reaches the heights of contemplation!

In these three things (which are the sign of love in its most perfect form) the utmost perfection of the Christian religion is undoubtedly found. I, by the grace of Jesus, and to the limit of my meagre capacity, have accepted them, yet I dare not equate myself with the saints who displayed them, because they understood such things so much more perfectly. However, let me press forward with all my strength so that my love becomes more fervent, my song more fluent, and my experience of love's sweetness all the fuller. For, my brothers, you are wrong if you suppose that people today cannot be as holy as the prophets and apostles were.

I call it *fervour* when the mind is truly ablaze with eternal love, and the heart similarly feels itself burning with a love that is not imaginary but real. For a heart set on fire produces a feeling of fiery love.

I call it *song* when there is in the soul, overflowing and ardent, a sweet feeling of heavenly praise; when thought turns into song; when the mind is in thrall to sweetest harmony.

This twofold awareness is not achieved by doing noth-

7. Aristotle, *The Physics*, 1, vii, 3.

ing, but through the utmost devotion; and from these two there springs the third, for unspeakable *sweetness* is present too. Fervour and song bring marvellous delight to a soul, just as they themselves can be the product of very great sweetness.

Now in all this richness is no trace of a false note, but rather the most exquisite perfecting of all our deeds. Not at all like those people who in their ignorance of the contemplative life are led astray by the *demon of noonday*[8] into a sham and fanciful devotion, because they consider themselves to have reached the top when in fact they are well down the scale. But the soul in whom are met these three things I have been speaking of remains completely impervious to the darts of the enemy; she continues to think all the time of her Beloved, rising ever higher, with her will unbroken, and her love stimulated. You must not be surprised if for such a soul, in her ordered love, there is melody and a continual retention through her Beloved of its music and comfort. For now she lives *no longer subject to vanity*,[9] but with heavenly support burns ever with uncreated, unfailing heat. And so, as I have already said, she loves ardently without ceasing, and feels within herself that supreme and gladdening heat, knowing she is simply burning with love's eternal fire. In her longing and sweetness she experiences her most Beloved; her meditation changes to a song of glory; and her very nature is renewed when she is caught up into this joyous song. Which is why her Maker has granted her her heartfelt desire: to pass without fear or grief from this decaying body, and to quit this world unafraid of death. For she who was the friend of light, and foe of darkness, loved nothing but life!

But men of this sort, who have been raised to such exalted love ought not to be chosen for positions of authority or for outward honour, or to be called to any kind of secular employment. They are stones like the topaz, found but rarely, and for that reason esteemed most precious. They are two-coloured: the purest colour is like gold, and

8. Psalms 91:6.　　　9. Romans 8:20.

the other is as clear as the cloudless sky. It surpasses the glory of every jewel, and nothing more beautiful can be seen. If we were to polish it we would make it dull, but leave it alone and it will retain its beauty. So the holy contemplatives mentioned earlier are the most rare and therefore the most dear of men. Like gold in their outstanding and fervent love, they are like the sky in the glory of their heavenly living. They surpass the life of any saint, and are the more beautiful and bright among the stones (I am speaking of course of the elect). They whose sole purpose is to love and possess this life shine more brightly than all other men, past or present. But if anyone wants to polish them, as it were, by loading them with honours, he will only diminish their ardour, and dull their beauty and brightness. And if they themselves accept public office and dignity, they do in fact demote themselves, and become less worth. So they ought to be left to engage in their own pursuits, in order that their brightness may continue to grow.

CHAPTER 15

How and when he was urged to the solitary life, and the song of love; about the change of place.

As adolescence dawned in my unhappy youth, present too was the grace of my Maker. It was he who curbed my youthful lust and transformed it into a longing for spiritual embrace. He lifted and transferred my soul from the depths up to the heights, so that I ardently longed for the pleasures of heaven more than I had ever delighted in physical embrace or worldly corruption. The way all this worked out, if I were minded to publish it, obliges me to preach the solitary life. For the inbreathing Spirit meant me to follow this life, and love its purpose. And this, from that moment, with all my limitations, I have sought to do. Yet I was still living amongst those who flourished in the world, and it was their food I used to eat. And I used to listen to that kind of flattery which all too often can drag the most doughty warriors from their heights down to hell itself. But when I rejected everything of this sort to set myself to one purpose, my soul was absorbed with love for my Maker. I longed for the sweet delights of eternity, and I gave my soul over to love Christ with every ounce of my power. And this she has received from the Beloved, so that now it is solitude that seems most sweet, and those comforts which in their madness men treasure are counted nothing.

From then on I continually sought quiet, and that although I went from one place to another. For to desert one's cell for reasonable cause does a hermit no harm any more than does its recovery if that seems right. Some of the holy Fathers were accustomed to do this, and thereby incurred criticism – but not from good men! For evil men spoke evil things, and would have gone on to do them if they had continued in the same place, for that is the way of them. Lift the lid of the pan, and there is only stink! Those who speak evil speak out of the abundance of their heart, and there lurks the poison of asps! I know this: the more men have been furious with me with their denigrations, the more have I advanced in spiritual growth. My worst detractors have been those I once counted my faithful friends. Yet I did not give up the things which helped my soul because of them, but got on with my study, always with the favour of God. I recalled the scripture which said, *They may curse, but you bless.*[1] And in the course of time I was granted growth in spiritual joy.

From the time my conversion of life and mind began until the day the door of Heaven swung back and his Face was revealed, so that my inner eye could contemplate the things that are above, and see by what way it might find the Beloved and cling to him, three years passed, all but three or four months. But the door remained open for nearly a year longer before I could really feel in my heart the warmth of eternal love.

1. Psalms 109:28.

I was sitting in a certain chapel, delighting in the sweetness of prayer or meditation, when suddenly I felt within myself an unusually pleasant heat. At first I wondered where it came from, but it was not long before I realized that it was from none of his creatures but from the Creator himself. It was, I found, more fervent and pleasant than I had ever known. But it was just over nine months before a conscious and incredibly sweet warmth kindled me, and I knew the infusion and understanding of heavenly, spiritual sounds, sounds which pertain to the song of eternal praise, and to the sweetness of unheard melody; sounds which cannot be known or heard save by him who has received it, and who himself must be clean and separate from the things of earth.

While I was sitting in that same chapel, and repeating as best I could the night-psalms before I went in to supper, I heard, above my head it seemed, the joyful ring of psalmody, or perhaps I should say, the singing. In my prayer I was reaching out to heaven with heartfelt longing when I became aware, in a way I cannot explain, of a symphony of song, and in myself I sensed a corresponding harmony at once wholly delectable and heavenly, which persisted in my mind. Then and there my thinking itself turned into melodious song, and my meditation became a poem, and my very prayers and psalms took up the same sound. The effect of this inner sweetness was that I began to sing what previously I had spoken; only I sang inwardly, and that for my Creator. But it was not suspected by those who saw me, for if they had known they would have honoured me beyond all measure, and I should have lost part of this most lovely flower, and have fallen into desolation. Meantime wonder seized me that I should be caught up into such joy while I was still an exile, and that God should give me gifts, the like of which I did not know I could ask for, and such that I thought that not even the most holy could have received in this life. From which I deduce that they are not given for merit, but freely to whomsoever Christ wills. All the same I fancy that no one will receive them unless he has a special love for the Name of Jesus, and so honours it that he never lets it out of his mind, except in sleep. Anyone to whom this is given will, I think, achieve this very thing.

From the time my conversion began until, by the help of God, I was able to reach the heights of loving Christ, there passed four years and three months. When I had attained this high degree I could praise God with joyful song indeed! And here that blessed state has remained since that initial impetus: and so it will continue to the end. In fact it will be more perfect after death, for though it is here that joyful love and burning charity begin, it is there, in the kingdom of heaven, that it will receive its most glorious fulfilment. But a man who has passed through these stages in his life profits to no small degree, yet he does not ascend to a higher stage, for he is one who has been confirmed in grace as it were, and so far as mortal man can be, is at rest.

I thank God that this is so, and I want to give him unceasing praise. In tribulations, in troubles, in persecutions, he has given me comfort; and in prosperity and success he makes me await in confidence his everlasting crown.

So, Jesus, I want to be praising you always, such is my
    joy.
When I was down and out you stooped to me,
    and associated me with those sweet ministers
    who through the Spirit give out those lovely and
      heavenly melodies.
I will express my joy and gratitude
    because you have made me like one of those
    whose superb song springs from a clear conscience.
Their soul burns with their unending love.
And your servant too, when he sits in prayer,
    glows and loves in his fervour.
His mind is transformed: he burns with fire;
    indeed, he expands in the vehemence of his longing.
And virtue, beautiful, true, lovely and faultless,
    flourishes before the face of his Creator.

His song suffuses his whole being,
 and with its glad melody
 lightens his burden,
 and brightens his labour.

God's gifts to us are manifold, wonderful and great, but none of them in this life can be compared with this one, which so perfectly confirms our hope in the beauty of the unseen life in the loving soul, and comforts him with its sweetness as he sits in prayer, and catches him up to the heights of contemplation, and to the sound of angels' praise.

And now, my brothers, I have told you how I came to the fire of love: not in order that you should praise me, but rather that you might glorify God. From him I have received whatever I have had of good. It is so that you who are aware that *everything under the sun is vanity*[2] might be moved to imitate, not denigrate.

CHAPTER 16

The prayer of the poor lover who desires to die; the praise of divine Charity.

WHEN a man, devout and poor, worries over his sin, he can pray (if he so desires) like this:

Jesus Christ, my Lord and God, take pity on me;
 please consider my body's grievous yoke,
 which depresses my soul so quickly.
My flesh is faltering under the burdens of life,
 and in consequence my spiritual strength is flagging too.
For all that the world ever gave me I have spent,
 and now nothing remains but for you to lead my soul
 to that other world where my most precious treasure,
 where my real and lasting wealth, abides.

2. Ecclesiastes 1 : 14 *et passim.*

There I shall live without wearying;
   there rejoice without grief;
   there delight without being sated;
   and there, loving you, seeing you, glorying in you,
   shall be satisfied for ever.
For truly my treasure is you, yourself.

Death, why do you delay? Why are you so slow in coming to me, a man alive but mortal? Why do you not catch hold of him who is longing for you? Who can possibly assess that sweetness which brings an end to all sighing, a beginning to all blessedness, the gate to a desired, unfailing joy? You are the end of my grief, you are the goal of my toil, you are the cause of my fruitfulness, you are the entrance to my joys. Yes, I burn, I pant for you. If you come I will be safe. Ravished though I be with love, yet I still cannot enjoy fully what I so desperately want; not until I taste that joy you are going to give me. For if I must, or rather because I must, like all my forbears, pass your gate, I beg you do not delay too long, do not be too far off. You can see how I am pining because of love, how I am longing to die, how I am aflame for you. Not, of course, for your sake, but for the Saviour's, my Jesus, on whom, once I have got what I want from you, I hope to gaze eternally. How good, Death, is the sentence you pass on this poor man, whose soul has been sweetened with love; on this poor man, moreover, whose love is for Christ, whose thoughts are heavenward, who burns sweetly with the fire of the Holy Spirit!

For this same poor man is taken after death to the place where angels sing, because he has been cleansed, and blessed, and now lives in the Spirit's music. He, who all his life has based his meditation on that lovely Name, will die surrounded by marvellous melody.

The hosts of heaven greet him with their hymns, and take him with honour to the court of the Emperor Eternal; there he will sit in blessedness among the inhabitants of heaven. Love brought him to the state in which he lives with such interior delight, and joyfully bears whatever may happen, and thinks on death not with anxiety but with pleasure. For he believes that it is then that he will truly live, when it is granted to him to pass from the light of this world.

Sweet charity, you are so obviously the dearest of all that is sweet! You take hold of our minds by your love; you possess them so clearly; you make them despise so quickly things that are transient, and pleasures that are vain; you cause them so remarkably to yearn for the things you want. You came to me ... and every secret corner of my heart has been filled with the lovely sound of your joy, and made abundant with fervent, spiritual happiness. Not surprisingly then, I long for love, the fairest of flowers, and inwardly burn with fiery flame. If only I could be quit of this place of exile!

The heat is such that no one can imagine it unless he has experienced its comfort for himself. His heart is bursting with song, a captive in the care of charity. For of all the things I experience here, this is the most delightful: I nearly die while it builds up its fervent love. Now my Beloved, grant that I may cease to live; for death, dreaded by so many, will be as the sound of music to me. And though I am now physically sitting in solitary state, I seem to be seated in Paradise, there singing sweetly my song of love for the joys my Beloved has given me!

CHAPTER 17

How perfect love is acquired by purity and affection; imperfect love; beauty; the threefold strength of divine love; rich men, poor men, and almsgiving.

IN a truly loving mind there is always a song of glory and an inner flame of love. They surge up out of a clear conscience, out of an abundant spiritual joy, out of inward gladness. Small wonder if a love like this wins through to a perfect

love. Love of this sort is immense in its fervour, its whole
direction Godwards, totally unrestrained in its love for him.
It cleaves to Christ without the opposition of silly thoughts;
it rejoices day and night in Jesus, never distracted from
him, never seduced by evil, never deceived by 'dead flies', or
driven off by them from the fragrance of the ointment.[1]
The world, the flesh, and the devil leave him unmoved,
however violent their attacks; he tramples them underfoot,
accounting their strength nothing. There is no tension in
his fervour, but there is vigour in his love; there is sweetness in his song, and a warmth about his radiance; his delight in God is irresistible, his contemplation rises with un-
impeded ascent. Everything he conquers; everything he
overcomes; nothing seems impossible to him. For while a
man is striving to love Christ with all his might he knows it
to be true that within him is eternal life, abundant and
sweet.

For we are in fact turned to Christ when we strive to love
him with all our mind. For, as subject, God is so wonderful
and, as spectacle, so entrancing, that it amazes me that any
one can be so stupid and perverse as not to want with all his
heart to see him.

It is not the one who does many things and great who is
great; but the one who loves Christ much: he is great, and
beloved of God. Philosophers have laboured much, yet they
have completely disappeared, and many who seemed to be
Christian, doing great things and performing great wonders, have not been found worth saving. Not doers, but
lovers of God are rewarded with the heavenly crown.

> I ask you, Lord Jesus,
>> to develop in me, your lover,
>> an immeasurable urge towards you,
>> an affection that is unbounded,
>> a longing that is unrestrained,
>> a fervour that throws discretion to the winds!

1. Ecclesiastes 10: 1.

The more worthwhile our love for you,
    all the more pressing does it become.
Reason cannot hold it in check,
    fear does not make it tremble,
    wise judgement does not temper it.

There is no one more blessed than he who dies because he loves so much. No creature can love God too much. In everything else what is practised in excess turns to evil, but the virtue of love is such that the more it abounds the more splendid it becomes. A lover will languish if he does not have the object of his love near him. Which is why the Scripture says, *Tell my Beloved that I languish for love*,[2] as if it were saying, 'It is because I cannot see him whom I love; my very body is wasting away with the intensity of my devotion!'

Undoubtedly when a man is turned wholly towards Christ he is at first moved with real penitence, and this involves his giving up everything that panders to vanity. It is afterwards that he is 'seized' by this taste for eternal sweetness, which is going to make him sing joyously for God. This is exactly what Isaiah says, *I will sing to my Beloved*,[3] and the Psalmist, *In you is my song for ever*.[4] So it is not surprising that those who have lived in God's love, and are accustomed to this inner, sweet, and burning fire, are not afraid to face death, but rather pass from this present light, even with joy. And after death they will ascend with gladness to the heavenly realms.

It is the mental wound caused by the flame of divine love that is referred to in *I am wounded with love*. Similarly when one pines for love, and is carried away by it, one can say, *I languish for love*. For it is thus that a man regards his Beloved. He forgets himself and everything else for Christ's sake; and so he says, *Set me as a seal upon your heart*.[5]

For what is love but the transforming of the desire into the loved thing itself? Or if you prefer, love is a great longing for what is beautiful, and good, and lovely, with its

2. Canticles 5:8.   3. Isaiah 5:1.
4. Psalms 71:6.   5. Canticles 8:6.

thought ever reaching out to the object of its love. And when he has got it a man rejoices, for joy is caused only by love. Every lover is assimilated to his beloved: love makes the loving one like what he loves. But God (and, for that matter, his creature too) is not above or averse to being loved: rather, everyone admits to liking being loved, and finding pleasure in others' affection. People are not made sad by the fact of loving, unless the loved one is ungrateful or they despair of obtaining the object of their love. Such disappointments are never found in loving God, though they are met with often enough when it is a matter of loving the world – or women!

I would not venture to say that all love is good. There is a love which delights more in the creature than in the Creator, and prefers the pleasures of the visible to the splendours of the spiritual. This is evil and abhorrent, because it rejects a love which is eternal for something which is transient and impermanent. Yet perhaps even this is not wholly culpable, since its purpose is to love and be loved rather than to corrupt and be corrupted. For the more beautiful a creature is, so much the more lovable it is. There are some who take more pains over the salvation of those who are outwardly more beautiful than of those who are despised, because for the beautiful there are more occasions of evil. Nature itself teaches us that it is more pleasant to love what is beautiful, though a disciplined charity says we should prefer the good. All physical beauty is straw, and disappears like a puff of wind. But goodness persists, and God often chooses the things that are weak and despised,[6] paying no heed to the powerful or lovely. This is what the psalm says, *He has delivered his strength into captivity, and his glory into the enemy's hand.*[7] Elsewhere we read, *You trusted in your own beauty and played the harlot.*[8]

It is the nature of love to melt the heart (as, for example, *My soul melted when my Beloved spoke*[9]). For sweet love and a devout heart so dissolve in the divine sweetness that

6. 1 Corinthians 1:27–8.   7. Psalms 78:61.
8. Ezekiel 16:15.   9. Canticles 5:6.

the will of man is united with the will of God in a remarkable friendship. In this union there is poured into the loving
soul such sweetness of warmth, delight, and song that he who
experiences it is quite unable to describe it.

The nature of love is that it is diffusive, unifying, and
transforming. It is diffusive when it flows out and sheds the
rays of its goodness not merely on friends and neighbours,
but on enemies and strangers as well. It unites because it
makes lovers one in deed and will, and draws into one Christ
and every holy soul. He who holds on to God is one in spirit
with him, not by nature, but by grace and identity of will.
Love has also the power of transforming, for it transforms
the lover into his Beloved, and makes him dwell in him.
Thus it happens that when the fire of the Holy Spirit really
gets hold of the heart it sets it wholly on fire and, so to
speak, turns it into flame, leading it into that state in which
it is most like God. Otherwise it would not have been said, *I
have said, 'You are gods; all of you are children of the Most
High.'*[10]

For there are some whose love for each other is so great
that it almost seems there is but one soul in the two of
them. Yet he who is poor in this world's goods but is rich in
spiritual things is far removed from love of this sort. For it
would be quite extraordinary if the man who is receiving all
the time, and who is rarely or never in a position to give, ever
had a friend on whom he could entirely rely. Yet he who is
thus thought by others to be unworthy of devoted love has
a faithful friend in Christ. He can confidently ask him
whatever he wills. Where human aid is wanting, divine
assistance is undoubtedly at hand.

All the same it would be more useful to a wealthy man if
he chose for his special friend some poor saint, with whom
he was willing to share all his possessions, and give them
freely to him – even more indeed than the poor man might
want – and should love him affectionately as his best and
dearest friend. For Christ said *Make to yourself friends*[11] –
and he meant the saintly poor who are the friends of God.

10. Psalms 82:6; cf. John 10:34–5.　　　　11. Luke 16:9.

God freely gives to the lovers of such poor the joy of Paradise because of their love. I reckon that such a rich man would be well satisfied with his friendship. But nowadays the proverb is only too true which says 'The sea will be dry when the poor man has a friend'!

I have found that some wealthy men will only give food to those whom they consider poor; they are unwilling to give clothing or other necessary things, reckoning it enough if they give food. So they make friends who are only half-friends or part friends, not bothering whether their friendship is with the good poor, or the bad. And all the precious things that ought to be given away they reserve for themselves or their children. The saintly poor are no more beholden to them than they are to those other benefactors who have given them clothing or anything else. What is worst of all, to the wealthy the poor seem a very considerable burden!

CHAPTER 18

The praise and effectiveness of charity; the renunciation of the world; the taking up of the penitential life.

CHARITY is the queen of virtues, the loveliest star of all; that beauty of soul which produces all these effects in our soul. In other words it wounds her and makes her long for God; it intoxicates and melts her, beautifies her, gladdens and enkindles her. Its behaviour is orderly, its practice is admirable. Every virtue to be true virtue must be rooted in charity. A man can possess no virtue that has not been planted in this love of God. He who multiplies virtues or good works apart from the love of God might as well throw precious stones down a bottomless pit! It is quite clear that whatever the things are that men do, they will not contribute to ultimate salvation if they are not done in love for God and neighbour. Since love alone makes us blessed, we ought to be willing to lose our life rather than to sully love by thought, word, or deed. It is in this love that the warrior rejoices; in these things that the conqueror is crowned.

The Christian hugging earthly riches, or looking for comfort in worldly things, is only half a Christian. There is no total renunciation of possessions, and without that no one can attain perfection.

For when a man intends to love God perfectly he strives to have done with everything contrary to the divine love, whether outward or inward, which may hinder him from loving. To do this sincerely he has to exercise great diligence, because he is going to endure serious hardship in its execution. Yet ultimately he will find the sweetest rest in this thing he has been seeking.

We have heard that *the way is narrow that leads to life.*[1] This is the way of penance and few find it. 'Narrow' is what it is called, and called rightly; through it the flesh sheds its unlawful things and the worldly comforts; through it the soul is held back from degenerate delights and decadent thoughts; through it the soul is totally given over to love of the divine. Yet it is not often found among men, because scarcely any have taste for the things of God, but look for earthly joys, and find their pleasure there. So they have recourse to sensual lusts, and neglect the mental: they detest any way that would lead to spiritual well-being, and reject it as narrow and rough, and to their lust intolerable.

All the same a mortal man would do well to consider this: he will never attain the kingdom of heaven by way of wealth or fleshly delight and pleasure, especially when it is written of Christ, *it was necessary for Christ to suffer, and so enter into glory.*[2] If we *are* members of Jesus Christ, our Head, then we are going to follow him. If we love Christ, we ought to walk as he walked. Otherwise we are not members of him, being separated from our Head. And if indeed we are separated we ought to be very much afraid, because it means that we are joined to the devil, and at the General Judgement Christ will tell us, *I never knew you.*[3]

In fact he too entered heaven by the *strait gate* and

1. Matthew 7:14.   2. Luke 24:26.   3. Matthew 7:23.

narrow way.[4] How can we, wretched sinners as we are, desire
to exchange poverty for wealth, to indulge in all the delights
and flatteries which this world offers, to secure for ourselves
every trifle and luxury, and yet at the same time expect to
reign with Christ in the life to come?

Christ *though he was rich, for our sakes became poor,*[5]
and we, though we are poor, want nothing so much as to be
(or to seem to be) rich. Christ, though he was Lord of all,
was made the servant of all: and we, though we are worthless and useless servants, want to lord it over all. He, though
he was the great God, was made lowly man: and we,
though we are merely weak exiles, are puffed up with pride
as if we were gods. He lived among men that he might lead
us up to heavenly things: and we, all our life, desire earthly
things.

It seems quite evident that we do not love him, since we
do not conform our will to his, nor are we concerned to
implement what we ask for daily when we say *Thy will be
done on earth as it is in heaven.*[6] It is a waste of time for such
men to count on being heirs with the elect, since they do
not share in Christ's Redemption: we have been redeemed
by his Blood, yet they despise it by their wicked and foul
deeds. Of their own free will they enslave themselves to the
devil.

CHAPTER 19

*The beauty of the mind, the vanity of the world, the love of
God and neighbour, considered together. Can perfect love be
lost and obtained in this life?*

I F you delight in beauty you ought to know that this quality of your mind will cause you to be loved by the Supreme
Beauty, so long as you keep such delight unsullied for love
of him alone.

For all fleshly beauty is corruptible, weak, and contempt-
ible; it quickly passes – and it deceives its lovers. In this life

4. Matthew 7:14.   5. 2 Corinthians 8:9.   6. Matthew 6:10.

virtue involves an unswerving hold of truth, the scorning and trampling down of vanity.

All those visible things people long for are vain. On the other hand the things which cannot be seen are true, and heavenly, and eternal. Every Christian shows himself to be the elect of God in this way: he scorns earthly things as nothing, and he is wholly given over to godly desires, which yield him the secret, sweet, music of love, a sound never known by earthly love. All the while a man is beguiled by worldly lust he is far removed, alas, from any taste for heavenly joy. But not surprisingly the shining soul, tirelessly following Christ, and wholly intent on loving eternity, is wont to be filled with abundant sweetness. Even in this life of flesh it sings its joyful song as if it were living with angels.

Therefore if our love is pure and perfect, it means that whatever our heart loves is God. If indeed we love ourselves and all other lovable creatures for God, and only in God, what else are we doing but loving him both in ourselves and in them? For when God is loved by us with all our heart and mind, undoubtedly both our neighbour and every other lovable thing is loved as well – and quite right too. So if we pour out our whole heart to God, in love for him, and by that token are bound closely to him, what other love can we have?

For in the love of God is the love of our neighbour. Therefore as he who loves God cannot but love man, so in the same way he who loves Christ in truth, can be shown to love nothing but God in him. And whatever it is for which we are loved or do love, we refer it all to God who is the source of love. For he who commands that every man's heart should be yielded to himself, is also eager that every affection and movement of the spirit should be fixed in him. Indeed he who really loves God, feels there is nothing in his heart save God, and if he feels there is nothing else he *has* nothing else. Whatever he has he loves for God, and he loves nothing but what God wants him to love. Therefore he loves nothing but God, and thus all his love is God.

In fact the love of this man is a true love because he

conforms himself to his Creator, who formed everything for his own sake. So he too loves everything for God's sake. Indeed, when the love of eternity is truly kindled in our souls, all earthly vanity, all fleshly lust, is accounted the filthiest refuse. And the mind, which is now completely given over to devotion, and seeking only the good pleasure of its Creator, blazes up within itself by the fervour of its love quite remarkably. Gradually it grows and glows in spiritual good, and no longer travels the broad slippery slope which leads to death, but is lifted with heavenly fire to the life of contemplation, ever going onwards and upwards.

No one in this vale of tears is going to attain perfection in the contemplative life overnight. For, first of all, a man's heart must be set really on fire by the torch of eternal love, so that he feels it burn with love, and he knows his conscience melt with exceptional sweetness. Little wonder when a man is first made a true contemplative, and tastes the sweetness and feels the warmth, that he almost dies through excess of love! He is held tight in the embrace of eternal love, almost as though it were physical, because with unceasing contemplation, and with his whole heart, he is attempting to reach up to and see that indescribable light. In the end such a man will allow his soul no comfort unless it comes from God, for now he is longing for such, and to the end of his life here he knows he will so desire, crying out anxiously with the Psalmist, *When shall I come and appear before the face of God?*[1]

Here is perfection of love. However, whether this state of love once attained can ever be lost is not an improper question to ask. For all the while a man can sin, it is possible for him to lose charity. But to be unable to sin means that a man is not still on the way but has reached his fatherland. Therefore however perfect a man may be in this life he is still able to sin, and sin mortally. For the attraction of sin is never wholly extinguished in any pilgrim, as a matter of common experience. But if anyone were able not to be tempted or to lust, he would clearly belong more to

1. Psalms 42:2.

the heavenly state than to this life, for he could not do wrong if he could not sin! I just do not know if there is any such person living in the flesh, but, speaking for myself, *the flesh lusts against the spirit and the spirit against the flesh*[2] and though *I delight in the law of God according to the inner man*[3] my love is not yet so great as to extinguish lust completely.

Yet I think there is a degree of perfect love which once a man reaches he will never thereafter lose. It is one thing to be able to lose it; it is another always to hold on to it because one does not want to let it go, even if such were possible. But the perfect abstain as much as they can from everything which will destroy or hinder their perfection. Though their own free will remains they are filled with the grace of God, and by it they are continually moved to love and speak and do good – and to draw back from an evil mind or mouth or deed. When a man is perfectly converted to Christ, he will hold in contempt all things that are transient, but keep a tight hold on his longing for his Maker – as far as is given to mortals, who have to allow for the corruption of the flesh. And then, not surprisingly because of this vigorous effort, he sees with his inward eye heaven open, as it were, and all the inhabitants there. Then it is that he feels that warmth most sweet, burning like a fire. He is filled with wonderful sweetness, and glories in jubilant song. Here indeed is charity perfected, and no one can know what it is like unless he lays hold of it; and he who does never loses it, but lives in sweetness and dies in safety.

CHAPTER 20

The usefulness and worth of prayer and meditation.

To acquire and retain this stability of mind, continual prayer is a great help. If in intention it is truly founded, it will overthrow the strength of devils. For although God

2. Galatians 5:17.   3. Romans 7:22.

knows everything – even before we ask for anything he knows perfectly well what it is we are wanting to ask – there are many reasons why we should pray. For Christ gave us an example of prayer when he went up alone into the mountain, and spent the whole night there in prayer. Moreover there is the apostolic precept, *Pray without ceasing*[1]; *men ought always to pray and not faint*.[2] Also, we pray in order to acquire grace in this present life, and glory in the future. So it is said, *Ask and you will receive. Everyone who asks receives, and it is opened to him who knocks*.[3] Again, angels offer our prayers to God, and so help their fulfilment. Our thoughts and longings are, of course, open and clear only to God, yet angels know when saints think worthy, holy thoughts, and when their fire burns brightly with the love of eternal life. They know through God's revelation, and by watching their outward actions, because they can see that they are serving God alone. Which is why the angel said to Daniel, *You are a man of strong desires*.[4]

Again, it is through continual prayer that our soul is kindled with the fire of love for God. For God says through his prophet, *Are not my words as a burning fire, and as a hammer for breaking stones?*[5] And the Psalmist adds, *Your speech is a burning fire*.[6] There are many nowadays quick to reject the word of God spoken from the heart, and allow it no room. So they do not kindle with warm comfort, but stay cold, sluggish, and indifferent, even though they have made countless prayers and scriptural meditations. It is because they do not pray or meditate with a perfect heart. But on the other hand there are those who drive sloth away, and in no time at all are alight and burning with love for Christ. And so rightly the verse goes on, *and your servant loves it*.[7] He is on fire indeed, because *he has loved your word, Lord*, which means he has meditated on it, and lives according to it.

1. 1 Thessalonians 5:17.   2. Luke 18:1.   3. Luke 11:10.
4. Daniel 9:23 (Vulgate).   5. Jeremiah 23:29.
6. Psalms 119:140 (Vulgate).   7. ibid.

He has sought you, rather than yours,
   and he has received from you both yourself and yours.
Others serve you for what they get out of you,
   and they care too little for yourself.
They pretend that they want to serve you,
   but it is only to gain worldly honour, and to be famous
     with men.
But while they rejoice, they find very little, and lose a
    great deal:
   not only you and yours, but themselves and theirs.

Again, we ought to pray in order to be saved. So James exhorts, *pray for one another that you may be saved.*[8]

Or again, we must pray so that we do not ease up, but rather busy ourselves continually in good works. That is why it is said, *Watch and pray that you do not enter into temptation.*[9] We ought always to be praying, or reading, or meditating, and doing other useful things, so that our enemy never finds us idle. We must give the closest attention to *watching in prayer*[10] with all our powers, so that we do not fall asleep. Failures in this respect distract the mind and make a man forget his aim, and if they are serious can be enough to destroy the effect of devotion. But this devotion is felt by the mind of a man who prays, provided he prays with watchfulness, and care, and love.

CHAPTER 21

The contemplative life is more worthy and meritorious than the active; preaching and prelacy.

SOME people are doubtful as to which life is the more meritorious and excellent, the contemplative or the active. To many of them the active life seems more deserving because of the amount of good works and preaching it performs. But this is the mistake of ignorance, because they do

8. James 5:16.   9. Matthew 26:41.   10. Colossians 4:2.

not know what the contemplative life stands for. True, there are many actives who are better than some contemplatives. But the best contemplatives are superior to the best actives. So we say therefore that the contemplative life, taken in itself, is sweeter, nobler, worthier, and more meritorious in respect of its fundamental principle, which is delight in *uncreated good*; in other words it is because this is the life which loves God more ardently. Therefore, the contemplative life, if it is properly lived, issues in a greater love of God, and demands more grace, than the active life. There is in the contemplative life the basic principle which calls for a more fervent love than the active life affords; and because contemplatives are quiet in mind and body, they can savour the sweetness of eternal love more than others do. Actives, to be sure, serve God with their toil and outward activity, but they spend little time in inner quiet. And the the result is that they can only rarely and briefly know spiritual delight. On the other hand contemplatives are almost always enjoying the embrace of their Beloved.

But there are those who take an opposite line. They say, 'The active life is more fruitful, because it performs works of mercy, and preaches, and does other such things. Therefore it is more meritorious.' I say, 'No, because such works have their own accidental reward, which is the joy of the *created good*.'[1] Thus a man taken up into the angelic order could have what an actual member of the order of cherubim or seraphim could not have, namely, the joy of some created good which he had done in his lifetime, which the other (who is, say, unrivalled in his love for God) did not do. So it often happens that someone of less merit is good and preaches, and another, who loves much more, does not preach. Is he who preaches therefore better? No; the one who loves more is the superior and better, although the one who is less will have merit because of his preaching; a merit

1. The distinction between *uncreated good* and *created good* is one of the instances which show Rolle's grasp of scholastic theology. *Praemium essenciale: gaudium de bono increato. Praemium accidentale: gaudium de bono creato.*

the other does not have because he did not preach. It is
patent therefore that a man is not more holy or excellent
because of the outward deeds he performs. For God who
looks on the heart rewards the will rather than the deed.
Good works depend on the will, not the will on the works.
The more ardent a man's love, the more exalted his reward.
For there is in true contemplatives a certain sweet fervour
and an abundance of God's love, which because it abides in
them infuses them with joy and song, and ineffable pleasure. This is never found here in those who are actives, for
they do not set their minds solely on heavenly things so
as to deserve to rejoice in Jesus. Therefore the active life is
rightly put second, and the contemplative preferred both
for the present and the future.

In Solomon's litter the pillars were silver and the back-
rest gold.[2] Our episcopal 'pillars' are the strong supporters,
and good rulers of the Church. They are 'silver', because
in their conduct they shine out, and in their preaching
sound forth! The 'golden back-rest' however must mean
the contemplatives; on these, living in supreme quiet,
Christ specially lays his head. And they too deliberately rest in him. These are 'gold', because in the integrity
of their lives they are purer and more precious, and in the
fervour of their loving and contemplating more aglow. God
indeed predestines his elect to fulfil various ministries. It is
not given to any individual to hold every office, but each
one has what best suits his state. Which is why the Apostle
says, *To each of us is given grace according to the measure
of the gift of Christ.*[3] Some people give alms out of their
wealth rightly acquired; some defend truth even unto
death; some preach the word of God clearly and power-
fully; others show their preaching in their writings; some
perform great penances for God's sake, and put up with
wretchedness in this life; some through the gift of contemplation yield themselves wholly to God, and surrender
themselves completely to loving Christ. Undoubtedly
among all the states which exist in the Church it is those

2. Canticles 3:9.   3. Ephesians 4:7.

who have that particular gift who rejoice; they have become contemplatives of the divine love, so now they exult and sing – and deservedly so.

If any man could achieve both lives at once, the contemplative and the active, and sustain and fulfil them, he would be great indeed. He would maintain a ministry with his body, and at the same time experience within himself the song of heaven, absorbed in melody and the joy of everlasting love. I do not know if anybody has ever done this: it seems to me impossible to do both at once. We must not reckon Christ in this respect as an ordinary man, nor his blessed Mother as an ordinary woman. For Christ did not have wandering thoughts, nor did he contemplate in the way that saints in this life commonly do. He did not need to work at it as we need, because from the moment of his conception he saw God.

Small wonder then that jubilant song comes to us only after great effort in spiritual work, and we receive from heaven the sweetest of sounds. Then it is that we wish to remain in this quiet, so that we can altogether delight in its continuing sweetness. Let him who manages his active life well set about rising up to the contemplative. But let not him who has reached the supreme degree of contemplation in the manner we have described come down to the active unless perchance he is obliged to accept office in the Church, a thing which as far as I know has never, or scarcely ever, happened. But perhaps some contemplatives could be chosen for this if they are less imbued with loving warmth. For lesser saints are sometimes better fitted for ecclesiastical office than are greater ones, because for the matters of everyday business those unable to persevere quietly in interior longing are more suited.

CHAPTER 22

The fire of love purges vices and sins; the signs of true friendship.

WHEN the fire of love has really taken hold of the soul it cleans out all vice, it puts away the trivial and unnecessary, it creates beauty in every virtue. It has nothing to do with mortal sin, though venial sin may remain. Yet the emotion and devotion of divine love can be so ardent that it will burn up venial sins as well, even if one is unaware of their existence. For when a real lover of God is carried away with fierce and fervent longing for him, everything displeases him which hinders the vision of God. Though he is delighting in joyful song his heart is unable to express what he is savouring of heaven. So much does he languish in love.

The perfect never carry combustibles with them into the next life! All their sins are burnt up in the heat of their love of Christ. But lest anyone should think himself perfect when he is not, let him listen to what it means to have perfection in oneself.

This is the life of the perfect man: it means rejecting all care of worldly affairs; leaving one's parents and one's property for Christ; spurning all transitory things for the sake of eternal life; destroying the things of the flesh after prolonged toil; refraining from wanton and improper desires as much as possible; burning in love for the Creator alone; experiencing, after the bitter sorrow and tremendous effort of spiritual labour, the sweetness of heavenly contemplation; and thus (if on behalf of the privileged I may be allowed to speak) to be taken hold of, and pass through the joy of loving God to spiritual song, through contemplation to heavenly music, remaining sweetly in inner peace with all commotion done away.

Although he has reached the point where he finds no pleasure in outward activity, inwardly the man of God is rapt with the delights and music of eternal love expressed in melodious song and unspeakable joy. So little wonder if in his mind he enjoys the sort of sweetness that angels have in heaven, although to a less degree. In this way a man is made perfect, and does not need to be purged by fire after this life: the fire of the Holy Spirit burns in him while he is yet in the body.

Yet this perfect love does not make a man incapable of sinning, but no sin can persist in him because it is at once purged by the fire of love. Again, one who loves Jesus Christ like this does not say his prayers the same way as other men however righteous they may be, because his mind is raised to great exaltation and is rapt with love for Christ. He is taken out of himself into indescribable delight, and the divinest music floods into him. Consequently, when he is reciting prayers, he does so with a certain spiritual quality, lifting up his vocal prayers in melodies inaudible to human senses, but clearly heard by himself and God. For spiritual power and strength have overcome the burden of the flesh to such an extent that now he can really rejoice in Christ. His heart, transformed by the fire of love, actually feels the heavenly warmth, so that he finds it difficult to sustain the immensity of love so ardent: he fears he may melt away! But the mercy of God preserves him until his appointed time. God it was who gave him the power to love so much, and to say in truth, 'I languish for love.' Like the fiery seraphim he burns, and loves, and sings, rejoices, and praises, and glows. The more fervent he is in loving, the more acceptable does he become. Not only does he face death unafraid, but he is even delighted to die, for he says with the Apostle, *To me to live means Christ is my life, and to die is joy.*[1]

1. cf. Galatians 2:20; Philippians 1:21.

CHAPTER 23

Perfect love does not adulterate the love of God; why and what one must love; carnal love is blinding.

I F we do in fact give up the squalor of sin and the vices of this world, we will be loving nothing that is not God. For what else do we see to love in our neighbour if not God? We are not wanting to love anyone unless it is for God's sake, and then to love him in God. For how can God really be all in all if there remains in a man a love for something else? No man can have joy except from a good that is loved. Consequently the more a man loves God, the more he will find abundant joy in him: and not surprisingly, for the more ardent and determined our pursuit of an object, the more intense is our joy in attaining it. Now if the source of a man's joy is his possession of God, God is that true joy which none can have who seek anything other than God. Indeed, if I am looking for something for my own sake, and not making God the end of that desire, clearly I am giving myself away, and parading my secret guilt for all to see.

But God wants to be loved in such a way that no one else has a share in that love. For if your heart is divided, and shamelessly loves some other thing as well, be quite sure that your love has been rejected by God, who does not bother with halfhearted love. All or nothing he accepts, for it is all that he redeems. Indeed you would have been damned, body and soul, because of the sin of Adam your father. But God came down into the Virgin's womb to be made man and to pay the price which set you free, to deliver not only your soul from the power of the devil, but also to bless you, body and soul, at the end of time.

And therefore you have the precepts of eternal life; if you want to enter the kingdom which was lost and has been recovered by the blood of Christ you must keep the commandments of Christ. And in so far as you desire to attain full and perfect joy when you die, you must remember to love God with a full and perfect heart while you live. Otherwise if you are not given to loving God today, you will have tomorrow not the fullness of joy but everlasting torment. All the time your love is not wholly directed towards your Maker you are making it plain that you are loving one of God's creatures beyond what is honest and lawful. It is not possible for a rational soul to be without love while it is alive. It follows that love is the foot, so to speak, by which after its pilgrimage on earth it will be carried either up to God or down to the devil, to be subject there to him whom it served here.

Nothing is loved except for the good it contains or is thought to contain, whether real or apparent. This is the reason why those who love physical beauty or temporal wealth are deceived or, one could say, tricked. For in visible and tangible objects there does not really exist either the delight that superficially appears, or the glory that is supposed, or the fame that is pursued.

No neglect of his soul is more damnable than that of the man who looks at a woman to lust after her. For when the glance of the eye excites a man, soon he will start thinking about the woman he has seen, and such thoughts cause lust in the heart, and corrupt the inner being. Then suddenly he is blinded by the smoke of a destructive fire and prevented from seeing the sentence which the strict Judge will pass. For the soul is cut off from the sight of heavenly things by this unclean and evil love, and cannot fail to show outward signs of damnation. It sets it well-being in the realization of the uncleanness it has conceived. So immediately it conceives sorrow in its grievous desire, and deservedly brings forth wickedness. The more the man is mistaken about the great danger which besets his soul – and he tries not to see it! – the more quickly does he stumble into filthy delight. For the judgements of God are *far away out of his sight*.[1] The moment he begins to enjoy carnal pleasures he pays no

1. Psalms 10:5.

116

attention to the miserable pit into which he is falling. The sentence of God in such a case is that he who has by his own choice despised God and fallen into mortal sin, will be (against his choice!) condemned after this life. This is God's judgement. In the life to come he will be quite unable to protect himself against the jaws of hell, because in this life here he sunk himself in crime and sin whenever he could, never wanting to forsake them, or even beginning to do so.

CHAPTER 24

The filthiness of soft living; its danger; physical contact; the evil of avarice, and pointless pleasure.

WHEN a man refuses to marry out of a pure love for God and virtue and chastity, and then sets about living in continence, adorned with every sort of virtue, there can be no doubt that he acquires a great reputation in heaven. Just as here he loves God without ceasing, so there he will praise him without ceasing. Marriage, of course, is good in itself, but when men subject themselves to its bond in order to satisfy their lust, they turn what is good into something evil. And when they reckon they are making the 'progress' they intended, they are by the same token going rapidly downhill. As for the man who loves wedlock merely because he fancies he will get rich as a result, undoubtedly he is trying to loosen its reins by his lasciviousness. Abounding in licence and wealth, he boasts that he has found what 'helps' his vile flesh.

Moreover there are men so perverse that they are consumed by uncontrollable lust for their own wives for the sake of their beauty, and the more quickly the body is reduced by their strength, the more they give themselves to satisfy their carnal lusts. But even while they are enjoying their delights they are beginning to fail; while they flourish they perish. Busy 'finding fulfilment' in voluptuous lust, they are in fact exhausting most dreadfully their mental and physical powers.

There is nothing more dangerous, more degrading, more disgusting than that a man should exhaust his mind in love for a woman, and pant after her as if she were his 'blessed rest'. And after it is all over, small wonder that he begins to degenerate, because before it had happened he had striven for this 'supreme blessedness' with such great anguish. But he knows well enough afterwards, as he thinks over his swift pleasure and its lengthy discomfort, that he has gone wrong, shamefully and senselessly wrong, in such love. For it is clear that he was tightly held by the evil bond of weak vanity. But not wanting to turn to God with all his heart, he did not recognize his wretchedness until he experienced it. So he fell into the pit, a captive, simply because he had no thought for the Throne of Glory. If he had known even a drop of the sweetness of eternal life, carnal beauty (that false, vain grace!) would not have seemed so sweet to his mind. But, alas, he does not consider how his wretched lust appears to the eyes of God Almighty, nor can he see himself as he really is in conscience, foul and revolting.

Again, no one can yield to the seductions of the flesh, without straying from the right path. For all the while the fire of earthly love inflames a man's mind, naturally enough the dew of divine grace evaporates, made useless and dry. Such love ever increases its heat, and from the fire of greed kindles the fire of sensuality, so that the crazed, enslaved soul most extraordinarily longs for nothing but carnal pleasures, and increased riches. It makes these things the purpose of its life: it burns because it must have them. It does not see the punishment which is the outcome, and to which it is rushing headlong. For the word of God, and his commandments, it cares nothing. Coveting only joys which are outward and visible, it is blind to those which are inward and unseen. And so it goes to the Fire with eyes tightly shut! And when the unhappy soul shall be free of its body, at once and for certain it will know at the Judgement how wretched it was while it lived in the flesh, though then it had thought itself to be both innocent and happy.

Therefore in whatever we do, we should always care more for cleanness of mind than cleanness of body. For it is a lesser evil to touch a woman's flesh with bare hands than to fill one's mind with evil longing. If in fact we do touch a woman, yet in heart think only what is good, clearly this ought not to be called 'sin', though because of this carnal temptation can sometimes arise. A man does not collapse in moral ruin when he keeps his mind fixed on God!

Yet when the heart of the handler is seized by all sort of sinful longings or is turned towards evil delights, and he does not check himself at once by love of his Maker or by firm virtue, you can be quite sure that that man has within him the sin of impurity, although in fact he may be far removed not only from any woman, but from any man too.

Moreover, if a believing man is married to an unbelieving wife it is likely that his own mind will be turned to unbelief. For it is the way of women when they sense they are loved by men above measure to proceed to beguile them by charm and flattery, and to lead them on to those things which their most wicked minds suggest, things which first they will have tried by open speech.

For Solomon was a wise man, and for some time was faithful to God. But later because of his too great fondness for female company, he most deplorably defected from faithfulness and from God's commandments. The man endowed with such great wisdom deserved to collapse grievously once he had allowed himself to be overcome by some foolish woman. When one hears that the wisest man can act so very unwisely no one is going to be so silly as to delude himself or to boast, 'I'm safe! I'm not scared! Worldly flattery is not going to trick me!'

Avarice, too, is another form of spiritual adultery, because the covetous man through his passion for money lays himself wide open to devilish prostitution. Before this excessive love of wealth he used to love God as his true spouse, but now he has deserted him through his inordinate greed, and has taken to himself wicked harlots. What is he committing if not fornication and idolatry? We must try therefore, to the best of our ability, to show a clean heart to the eyes of Almighty God, and to put paid to all those baneful pleasures. And if we have done anything at any time through frailty, at least let it be seen that in heart before God there is only that which is perfect and exalted. Sometimes people vilify us because we are too happy; sometimes our joy shows itself in the way we speak or look; and although this sort of thing can be done before God with a clear conscience, before man, as we well know, it is liable to be misunderstood. Therefore we have got to be sensible and take special care not to put ourselves into a position where we could unwittingly be a possible cause of evil.

For servants of Christ it is good to cling closely to God, because through longing for him they receive the fire of the Holy Spirit, and sing the delights of eternal love with the loveliest and sweetest sound of heaven. The heavens are made honey sweet: in other words, the saints love Christ all the more ardently the more they realize how much he has borne for them. For while the mind of the saints is set wholly on the love of eternity, they who are rapt with the sweetness of heavenly life glory in the fact that they have already savoured it and its melody on earth.

CHAPTER 25

Perfect love; what is necessary to obtain spiritual song; affection and correction.

THE splendour of our reward depends on the greatness of our love, and the one who loves very greatly burns with an unquenchable blaze, and is filled with heavenly sweetness. The more generous his love, the higher his standing in the Kingdom. But this love, however, is in the heart, and the more he loves God the more joy he experiences in him. They are wrong then who assert that he who has only ex

perienced the joy of love occasionally or briefly loves
much as does the man who all day long is as it were sate
with sweetness. Some find it hard to love, others easy, but
the love of God is more blessed when it is easier; being
easier makes it more fervent; more fervent means sweeter;
sweeter greater. It is greater in men who live quietly than in
those who toil. So they who continue in quiet, love the more
fervently. They are superior to those who sometimes are
given to quiet, and sometimes are busy about outside jobs.

Nothing is better than mutual love, nothing sweeter than
holy charity. To love and be loved is the delightful purpose
of all human life; the delight of angels and of God, and
the reward of blessedness. If then you want to be loved, love!
Love gets love in return. No one has ever lost through
loving good, if he has persisted in love to the end. On the
other hand he does not know what it is to rejoice who has
not known what it is to burn with love. So no one is ever
more blessed than the man who is transported out of himself by the vehemence of his love, and who through the
greatness of God's love experiences for himself the sweet
song of everlasting praise. But this does not happen to a
man overnight unless he has been converted to God, and
has made remarkable efforts, and has rejected every desire
for worldly vanity. Normally God infuses his own indescribable joy into those who love him. For a mind ordered
and clean receives from God its thoughts of eternal love.
Thinking has been cleansed when it is surging up into
spiritual song. Purity of heart deserves to have the sound of
heaven; and so as to maintain the praise of God with joy
the soul is kindled with divine fire, and made glad with
ineffable sweetness.

A man who gives up this world completely, and attends
closely to reading, prayer, meditation, watchings, and fastings, will gain purity of mind and conscience, to such an
extent that he would like to die through his supernal joy,
for he longs *to depart and to be with Christ*.[1] But unless his
mind wholeheartedly cleaves to Christ, and he longs for

1. Philippians 1:23.

him constantly and deliberately in all his thoughts, thoughts which are wholly loving and in intention unending, thoughts upon which he meditates unceasingly wherever he sits or wherever he goes, seeking interiorly to love only Christ, he will certainly not know any heavenly song, or sing joyfully to Jesus, or sound his praises either mentally or aloud.

Pride indeed is the downfall of many, for when they think they have done something which others are not accustomed to, at once they put themselves forward and quite improperly snub those who could well be better than they. But let them realize this: that man does not know love who presumes to despise what is common to himself and his neighbour. He injures his own case who does not acknowledge the right of another, and he violates the law of common humanity because he does not respect his bond with his neighbour. It is in this way that men stray from the love of God, and they do not know how to attain it because they do not give themselves to love their neighbour as they ought. Him they dismiss as altogether sinful and wrong, or if they begin to correct or rebuke him they speak with such asperity and harshness that they often make him worse by their correction.

They should speak with gentleness, so as to win him by soft words. Unbridled correction only makes matters worse.

CHAPTER 26

The sighs, vows, and humility of the perfect lover; the dissimilarity between love of the world, and love of God; meditation.

THE voice of the soul longing with eternal love and seeking the beauty of her Maker, rings out. *Let him kiss me with the kiss of his mouth,*[1] it says; in other words, let him delight me in union with his Son. Faint with love, I long with

1. Canticles 1:2.

my whole heart to see my Love in all his beauty. But meanwhile may he visit me with his sweet love as I toil and struggle on through this pilgrimage. And may he turn my heart to himself so as to delight me with the warmth of greater and greater love. Until I can see my Beloved clearly I shall sing at every remembrance of his sweet name; it is never far from mind.

He who delights to do what his Saviour wishes not surprisingly finds delights in this present world as well. Nothing is more pleasant than praising Jesus; nothing more delectable than hearing him. For hearing rejoices my mind, and praising lifts me to himself. And when I am deprived of these things I sigh in my need, for then I hunger and thirst, and know myself bereft. Yet when I feel the embrace and caress of my Sweetheart I swoon with unspeakable delight, for it is he – he whom true lovers put before all else, for love of him alone, and because of his unbounded goodness!

And when he comes, may he come into me, suffusing me with his perfect love. May he refresh my heart by his continual gifts, and by removing every hindrance to his love make me glow and expand. Who will dare to say that a man is going to fall into the foul filth of the flesh, if Christ has deigned to refresh him with the heavenly sweetness of celestial vision? This is why such a man sings sweetly something like this, 'We will rejoice as we remember *your breasts that are better than wine,*[2] as if to say,

'We are wanting your honour, your glory:
   we are rejoicing in your delights.
The pleasures and plenty of passing vanity
   have been put away,
    things which so bemuse those who love them,
    that they cannot see the evils they will suffer.
And although as yet we cannot see your Face
   our longing is still so ardent
    that were we to live for ever thus

2. Canticles 1 : 1 (Vulgate).

we would seek no other object of our love.
The longer we live the more fervently we want you,
　　and the greater joy we experience in your love.
We sigh earnestly for you.
Things cease to be unpleasant when men love you,
　　and they become happy and joyful.
For the soul that truly loves you, Jesus,
　　would rather die the most awful death
　　than consent to sin, however little.'

A man's love for Christ is not true or perfect if he is
afraid of anyone else. *All things work together for good to
those who love God.*[3] Love that is perfect conquers pain
and overcomes threats, because it is afraid of no one. It
rejects the proud, yet in its humility yields place to all. It is
truly said, *The righteous love you,*[4] for the righteous are
humble, and love in truth, and do all the things they should.
Though they live in high perfection, in thought and deed
they bear themselves in great humility. And so each true
lover may say to himself, 'All men are better than I in their
contempt of the world, their hatred of sin, their desire for
heaven, their sweet and fervent love for Christ, their charity
towards their neighbour. Some abound in virtue, some
glitter with miracles, some are exalted with the heavenly
gift of contemplation, some search out the secrets of Scripture. When I think of the worthy lives of such people in
comparison with my own I am reduced, as it were, to nothing: I give way to the very lowest.'
The righteous are those who deliberately run away from
earthly hindrances, for they pant only after everlasting joys.
All appetite for transient things fades, and they run after
the love of God with urgent longing. Quite properly they
are said to love God, for they go by the right, straightfor-
ward way of shining charity, and have no taste or longing
for anything but Christ. They do not resemble those mentioned by the Psalmist, *Let their eyes be blinded so that
they cannot see, and ever bow down their backs,*[5] referring

3. Romans 8:28.　　　4. Canticles 1:3.　　　5. Psalms 69:23.

124

to those who cling to earthly things, and make eternal things second to transitory. Which is why the wrath of God is poured out upon them, and justice is vindicated in the great and violent torments which overwhelm them.

For without pause the righteous aim at enjoying the vision of God, and this they do with heart and voice and effort, all pretence put away. They do not turn aside to love pointless vanity lest they be deflected in their pilgrimage from following the path of righteousness. When a man wants to please Christ he will not do anything, good as well as bad, contrary to Christ's will. It is indeed ghastly to go down into the fires of Gehenna, but more hateful still to want to sin for one's own pleasure. In this way one can lose Christ for ever!

The soul that is truly separated from vice, and is a stranger to venal and carnal sweetness, the soul that is wholly given to heavenly desire, and is enthralled thereby, enjoys quite remarkable pleasure because she is in some way experiencing the delight of her Beloved's love. Now she is able to contemplate more clearly, and her pleasure is all the keener. Now is the time when she demands her Spouse's most gracious lips, and his sweetest kiss. 'All earthly things I despise,' she cries, 'I know how much I love my Beloved, I am aware of his most wonderful comfort, I yearn for his sweetness, I am not going to fail now that the greatest temptations have been put behind me. Love is making me bold to summon my Beloved that he might comfort me, come unto me, and *kiss me with the kiss of his mouth.*[6] For the more I am raised above earthly thoughts the more fully do I enjoy the pleasure I long for; the more carnal longings are banished, so much the more truly do the eternal ones flare up. Let him kiss me and refresh me with his sweet love; let him hold me tight and kiss me on the mouth, else I die; let him pour his grace into me, that I may grow in love.' Children are fed and nourished with mother's milk; and elect souls, blazing with love, are fed with supernal delights, and so led on to the vision of the everlasting Glory.

6. Canticles 1:1.

To be sure, the delights of loving Christ are sweeter than all the tasty pleasures of the world and the flesh. Indeed, unimaginable carnal pleasure, and abundant earthly possession, in comparison with the minutest sweetness poured by God into an elect soul are paltry and appalling!

> Vast as the difference may be
> between the sum total of earthly wealth
> and the greatest depth of worldly poverty,
> so the sweetness of your love, my Beloved,
> is infinitely greater
> than all those delectable earthly joys
> the lustful thirst after,
> and the worldly live for,
> and in which alone they glory.
> They have no experience of that love of yours
> which ought to be their delight.

But spiritual gifts oblige the devout soul to love fervently, to meditate sweetly, to contemplate deeply, to pray joyfully, to praise worthily, to long for Jesus and him only, to cleanse the mind from the filth of sin, to quench the desires of the flesh, to despise all things of earth, to have a mental picture of the cross and wounds of Christ, and with tireless longing to pant and sigh for the vision of that most glorious purity. These are the ointments best suited for beautifying the soul who is dedicated to the love of God.

CHAPTER 27

True humility; the way of benefiting by adversities, and the examples of the saints; meditation on the Passion of Christ.

HUMBLE men do not look at other people's sins but at their own, nor do they praise their own good deeds but those of others. The reprobate, however, do just the opposite, because they concentrate more on the evils of others than on their own, these latter being in comparison (they

say) either non-existent or trivial. But their own good deeds
– assuming there are any – they prefer to anybody else's,
whose goodness indeed they are anxious to play down when
they cannot altogether dismiss it.

But there are two things which it hurts me to hear. The
first is when I, wretched I, have known myself praised when
I ought properly to have been despised. The second is when
I see my neighbour whom I have loved in God, and for God,
slandered and denigrated. Nevertheless, you who are giving
up the world in the attempt to follow Christ in his path of
poverty must strive to know yourself. Because if you do in
fact renounce the greeds and deeds of this day and age, you
are binding yourself for Christ's sake to bear cheerfully the
rebuffs of the world, and with all your might to run away
from riches. Were you to be unaware of this, and give no
heed to it, you would be led astray and away from the love
of Christ.

Do not be surprised therefore if you are worn out with
troubles of every sort, or are attacked by a variety of
temptations. Withstand them unmoved, and you will be
sweeter and dearer in the sight of God. Remember that *he
proves them as gold in the furnace is proved.*[1] Those who
know for themselves the sweet love of Christ can embrace
tribulation gladly, because they are not seeking any outward consolation at all. Such is the sweetness poured into
the mind of the true lover of Christ that if all the pleasures
of the world were to be put together in one place he would
still run off into the wilderness, rather than cast even a
single glance at it. To such a man the sum total of earthly
comfort seems desolation rather than consolation; for a soul
regularly visited by God's love and joy just cannot feed
itself with empty glory. His heart never leaves his Beloved,
and he would rather die than even once offend his Redeemer.

But that you also may obtain this grace, keep well in
mind the examples of sinners who repented, and try to
imitate the life of the saints. Then you who also are a

1. Wisdom 3:6.

sinner (though converted to the service of God) may get a glimmer of hope through the example of sinners who have been raised to his Kingdom, and by studying the lives of the righteous may keep yourself from undue elation! It is by the recollection of these better things that the holy man becomes humble. Because whoever it is that you find described or written about, you can always reckon that he is incomparably more worthy than yourself. It is such people who are called the lovers of Christ: those who for his sake get the knocks and blows of the world; who because they despise wealth and empty glory are subjected to contempt, insult and slander; whose very praise is torture to them. Yet they live as solitaries, for God's sake, living a dying life – and they are taken up to the company of angels in their fatherland!

I myself fled to the wilderness when it proved no longer possible to live harmoniously with men, who, admittedly, were a frequent obstacle to my inner joy. Because I did not do the kind of things they did, they attributed waywardness and bad temper to me. But *when I found trouble and heaviness, I called on the name of the Lord*.[2]

But lest we give way through temptations let us make it our aim to let earthly coveting go, and to keep the crown of eternal glory firmly before our mind. And then, as we have been found watchful, we will receive the promised blessedness. But in the meantime we take whatever steps we can to ensure that carnal lust is held in check at source, and the heart, most sensibly, relinquishes its physical greed, so that in the service of God our body can stand firm and strong.

The man who really gives up everything for love of Jesus, who lets go the will to possess, both stands fast and benefits through this. He will own joyfully that *he has found what his soul loves*.[3] For Christ is found in the heart warmed by eternal love – and that warmth is longing to be sought out, and no mistake!

For Christ comes down into the soul with a warmth of honeyed sweetness, and with a joyful song, and he who

2. Psalms 116:4. 3. Canticles 3:4.

experiences this can boldly say, 'I have found my Love.' The man who in his prayer sees his mind really lifted out of itself and raised beyond the material heaven (assuming of course that he does not give up but yearns more and more for the taste of eternity) can cheerfully wait for the mercy of Christ, for in a few short years he knows he will be caught up to contemplate glory. So with humble heart he keeps going and ceases not till he reaches the fellowship of everlasting rest.

But if in your prayer your inner eye is ravished by contemplating heavenly things, the time is near when your soul, risen above earthly matters, is going forward in the love of Christ. But the man who prays without being raised to things supernal will be wise not to stop meditation, prayer and vigil until he sees these higher things. Else he will grovel, feeling himself despised, in anguish and affliction.

Go forth, daughters of Sion, says the Scripture, meaning 'you souls who are newborn', *and see King Solomon crowned,*[4] meaning 'understand Christ is truly our peace, for he suffered for our salvation. Gaze at him, and you will see that divine head crowned with thorns, his face spit-covered, those clear eyes languid and wan, his back scarred with flogging, his breast bare and bleeding, his venerable hands transfixed, his dear side pierced with the spear, his feet nailed through, and all that tender flesh marked with wounds, as it was written, *from the sole of the foot to the crown of the head there is no health in him.*[5] Leave then, leave your illicit lusts, and see what Christ suffered for you, so that your sins can clearly be cast away, and your hearts taught to burn with love.'

4. Canticles 3:11. 5. Isaiah 1:6.

CHAPTER 28

The true lover spurns earthly things, and sighs for eternal;
the avoiding of pride, and the embracing of humility.

SEE, wretched little man, how the delights of carnal lust cover up the terror of the coming damnation! Which is why you must withstand them, because they seek to take away virtues, things that belong to Christ. For before your heart can burn with the love of Christ it will have to get rid of its appetite for all passing vanity whatever. A mind on fire with the spirit of Christ finds its sole nourishment in its love of eternity, and its gladness in joyful song.

If the sweetness of eternal love is present in your soul, undoubtedly it will destroy lascivious and carnal wickedness. It does not allow you who delight in Christ to know anything but Christ, because now you cannot fall from him or know any other sweetness than his. The perfect, indeed, when they die are duly presented to God, and are sat down in the seats of blessed rest, because they see Christ to be God, and they are in peace.

Those who really begin to love Christ will subsequently have great and loving joy and honey-sweet fervour, and will never cease in their love-songs to the Lord Jesus. No earthly thing can possibly please the man who truly loves Christ, since because of his great love he can find no value in anything merely passing. Though the righteous see physical things, of course, with their bodily eye, they are in fact looking at celestial things with hearts humble and clean. They are alight with the flame of the heavenly vision, and know themselves free from the burden of sin, and now no longer sin in their wills. The heart that has turned to fire, embraces nothing of the world, but strives always to pierce heaven.

Those indeed who are destined for holiness, at the outset of their conversion give up their evil crimes and worldly vanities through fear of God; next they subdue their flesh by severe penance; and then, when they have put the love of Christ before all else, they taste something of the delight of heavenly sweetness and progress rapidly in devotion of soul. So they mount up, step by step, abounding in spiritual virtues; and thus are made beautiful by the grace of God, to come at last to the perfection which affects heart, speech, and toil.

But he who has been absorbed by the love of Christ is made dead as it were to the attraction of outward things; he is savouring and seeking *the things that are above and not the things of earth*.[1] It is no surprise that in his mind he sighs as he longs for the heavenly Kingdom, or that he grows in his love for the Bridegroom, or that he rejoices in deep interior happiness, or that he loses his passion for worldly things, or that he is full of longing for his true love, his whole mind bent on seeing God in his beauty. Ablaze with flaming love for God, he wants only what God desires, and he himself desires nothing save God. For when a faithful soul longs most fervently only for the presence of the Bridegroom, she is completely frigid towards all lascivious and empty glory. And so she pines for love, because she holds everything earthly as nothing; and she sighs, while she hastens on to the everlasting joys.

He who delights himself in Christ's love, and longs to have this consolation continually, not only does not seek human solace, but even flees from it most strenuously, as if it were smoke hurting his eyes. For just as air is suffused by the sun's rays and becomes itself splendid with the splendour of its light, so the devout mind, inflamed by the fire of Christ's love and filled with desire for heavenly joys, seems to be all love. It is totally transformed into something different, indescribably delightful, though it retains its fundamental essence. For when the mind is kindled by the fire of the Holy Spirit, it is liberated from all idleness and uncleanness. It is made sweet in the torrent of God's love, for it is always looking at him, and not considering earthly

1. Colossians 3:2.

things at all, until that day when it is glorified with the perfect vision of its Beloved.

But one must beware of pride and a spiritual swelled head, because this can throw the most noble of men into profound dejection. For what is more loathsome, or deserving of punishment, what is more worthless and abominable, than that the most despicable worm, the worst sinner, the lowest of the low, should swagger about and exalt himself here on earth, this world for which the King most high, the Lord of Lords, condescended to humble himself? If you were to consider Christ's humility deeply, whatever your own background or wealth or virtue, not in your self would you find reason for pride, so much as cause to despise yourself – and then, humility. You, therefore, the despiser of sinners, look at yourself lest you are in fact making yourself worse than other people, for a proud righteous man displeases God more than does a humble sinner.

But when true humility has taken root in your mind, whatever good you do is done in praise of your Maker, so that you despise your own virtue and seek his glory, lest you succumb to vanity and lose your everlasting reward.

Think therefore of Jesus with a longing heart; let your prayer go out to him; let it continually seek him; your only care be to possess him. Happy the rich man who has such a possession! For this, let go all the emptiness of the world; he will conquer your enemy and bring you to his kingdom.

The devil who assails you will be overcome, the flesh which is so aggravating will be subdued, the world which tries to deceive you will be despised – all this, if your heart does not give up its quest for the love of Christ.

That man is not sitting idle who in his heart is crying out to Christ, however silent his tongue might be; for there is no physical rest for the body when the mind is tirelessly desiring heavenly things. The man who persistently and always covets eternal things will not be thought lazy. The thoughts of a lover of Christ rise upwards swiftly and smoothly. They do not allow themselves to go after passing things, or get involved in carnal matters, but they go on and up until they reach the heavenly places.

For sometimes when the body is tired in the service of Christ, the spirit is exalted, and the mind is caught up to heavenly refreshment and, indeed, to the contemplation of God. For he who prays devoutly does not have a heart which wanders about in worldly things, but one that is transported to God in heaven. He who wants to have what he prays for pays careful attention both to the subject-matter of his prayer, to the one he is addressing, and to the reason he is making it, so that he may love him to whom he prays, lest like some outcast he is asking in vain for a reward from life.

The saints, however, are so profoundly humble that they believe themselves to know nothing and to achieve nothing. Their claim is that they are more worthless and wretched than anybody else, worse even than those they correct and chastise! In obedience to the Lord's command they take the lowest seat, yet that lowly seat of theirs receives not rebuke from God, but honour: not demerit or the denigration of their merits, but the reward of praise and promotion to splendour. To this humility best disposes! For that very humility brings praise to Christ, torment to the devil, and glory to the people of God. It makes the servant of Christ love more ardently, serve more devotedly, praise more worthily; and it produces a fuller degree of charity. The more a man humbles himself the more does he promote the praise of God. He who really perseveres in loving God and his neighbour, and yet in his humility and self-knowledge reckons himself to be of no value and inferior to others, will conquer his enemies, have a confident hope in the love of the great Judge, and when he passes from the light of this world be received by angels into eternal joy.

CHAPTER 29

Instruction for the simple and beginners who are eager to love; the avoiding of women.

THE faithful soul, bride of Jesus Christ, rejects pride because she loves humility so profoundly. She abominates vainglory because her only desire is for eternal joy and to follow Christ. She loathes carnal pleasure with its softness because she is already tasting the sweetness of eternity, and is burning to have for ever the love of the Beloved. There is no bitterness or resentment about her because through her love for Christ she is ready to endure anything. Indeed, she does not even know how to be envious of other people, since, radiant with real love, she rejoices in the progress and salvation of everybody.

As a matter of fact no one is ever jealous unless he is in truth less than the larger size he thinks himself to be! Such a man will heap insults on people lest they should seem equal to himself! But if anyone is said to be more important, beautiful, or strong, he at once becomes terribly jealous and dejected. But a soul which has been kindled however slightly by the fire of the eternal vision does not look for empty glory and passing praise. It is obvious that men who backbite and are envious of each other do so because they have no love for God – unlike God's elect. Where they are who love God, there too are men as eager for the good of their fellows as they are for themselves. So if you want to love God supremely, learn to abominate all earthly praise. For Christ's sake embrace the contempt of man and his mockery – and brace your mind for the everlasting sequel! You would choose rather to experience fiery torment with the reprobate in hell, than to have any part with them in sin. For the man who loves Christ ardently, and rejoices and sings in the sheer delight of that love, is the one who lives secure and sure. To him it would seem more pleasant to fall into the flames of eternity than to commit just one mortal sin! Such are the saints, for they live purely, despise all worldly things, and now sing melodiously what once they could only say – such is their fervour and spiritual joy. They burn with love for Christ, their eyes are set on heaven, and to the utmost of their power they occupy themselves with good works; they abound in the delights of everlasting life, yet to themselves they seem the vilest of men, and the lowest and worst of all.

Therefore you who till now have been uncouth and ignorant must make every effort to withstand your spiritual enemies, and not allow any wrong thought to find room in your heart. Set your wisdom against the wiles of the devil. When some unclean imagination or thought has obtruded itself against your better judgement, do not yield to it, but fight it manfully, and cry unceasingly to Christ until you are clothed with God's armour. If you want to imitate those who despise the world, never think about what you are giving up, but what you are despising, with what devotion you are presenting your vows to God, with what longing and love you offer your prayers, with what fervour you yearn to see God, and to be united to him. If you truly hate all sin, if you do not hanker after passing things, if your soul refuses to comfort herself with earthly consolation, if you savour things supernal, if you crave to contemplate heavenly things (and supremely the Son of God), if your speech is controlled and wise – for whoever's spirit is absorbed in the sweetness of loving God and singing to Jesus does not speak unless obliged to – by such means and such training you will reach perfection.

It is not surprising that God should approve one who in this way despises the world. The soul, made sweet through her shining conscience, and beautiful through her love of eternal charity, can be called 'the garden of Christ'; for when the vices have been weeded out she flowers with virtue and rejoices with joyful song – like the singing of birds! We must, then, give all diligence to obeying God, to serving him, to loving him, and in all our good works our purpose must be to attain to him.

For what is the point of wanting earthly things, or desiring carnal love, if the only lasting result is the wrath of the Judge, and everlasting punishment? For carnal love inevitably excites temptations; it blinds the soul from following real purity; it hides the sins that have been committed, and foolishly precipitates new wrongs; it inflames the soul with every sort of depraved delight. Moreover it troubles quiet of every kind, and hinders fervent love for Christ; it corrupts the virtues earlier won.

And so it follows that a man who honestly wants to love Christ must not let his imagination toy with the love of women. When women love, they love without reserve, because they do not know how to restrain their manner of loving. On the other hand loving them can be a very tricky and prickly business! One eye they keep on the main chance, and the other on genuine emotion. Loving women upsets the balance, disturbs the reason, changes wisdom to folly, estranges the heart from God, takes the soul captive, and subjects it to demons! And he who looks at a woman with natural affection yet not with lustful desire finds he is unable to keep free from illicit urges or unclean thoughts. Often enough he feels in himself the stain of filth and even may take pleasure in the thought of developing it.

Womanly beauty leads many astray. Desire for it can sometimes subvert even righteous hearts, so that what began in spirit ends up in flesh. So beware of entering into conversation with a woman just because she is lovely. You will be caught by the poisonous disease of pleasure, and, knowingly deceived, you will set about implementing your dirty thoughts. Fool that you are, you will allow yourself to be taken captive by your enemies. Be wise then, and flee from women. Do not ever think about them, because even if a woman is good, the devil's attack and his insinuations, the attraction of her beauty, and the weakness of your flesh can beguile your will beyond measure.

But if you brood ceaselessly on the love of Christ, and wherever you are keep it reverently before you, I warrant you will never be deceived by false female flattery. Indeed,

the more you see you are attracted and tempted by their
empty endearments, so the more you will despise them for
the stuff and nonsense that they are, and, not surprisingly,
the more richly you will rejoice in God's love.

For in those who love him Christ works in the most
wonderful fashion, and with tender, special love takes them
to himself. They have no desire for luxury or for physical
beauty, and they have consigned all transitory things to
oblivion; they do not care about worldly success, nor do
they fear opposition. They love especially to be alone, to
hasten unhindered towards the joy of knowing God's love.
Suffering for Christ seems to them something very sweet,
not very hard. If anyone wants to honour a martyr's triumph worthily let him show his devotion to his virtue by
his imitation of it; let him share the martyr's cause even if
he does not have to submit to his pain; let him persist in
patience, for in so doing he will have complete victory.

The soul which gives up the folly of evil love enters upon
the narrow way. It is on this way that the foretaste of the
life of heaven is experienced. The consolation felt is such
that it overcomes all delight in passing things; the soul asks
her Beloved to grant his comfort and inner refreshment,
and to pour in the grace of perseverance lest she be fatigued
by her errors, and falter. So when a young man begins to do
well let him always remember that he must persevere and
never drag his feet or give up his good purpose. Mentally at
least let him always advance, and rise from lesser to greater
things. When he has rejected even the shadow of error and
has spurned with contempt the sweet poison of lawless living he will lay hold of the narrow life and embrace the
sweetness of a life devoted to God. Thus step by step and
helped by the Holy Spirit's gifts within him he climbs the
heights of the contemplation of God. He is refreshed and
delighted by the warmth of everlasting love, and in this
heavenly joy he abounds – up to the very limit possible for
mortal man.

To be sure, the beloved soul who is troubled on every side
and tormented by raging temptation is unable to savour the

sweetness of love as it is in itself. Yet she has experienced its joy, and she keeps steadily reaching out to her Beloved. It is quite possible not to have this marvellous sweetness, but she loves Christ with such longing that she keeps going for love of him alone.

How greatly ought we to praise this most generous help! Every true lover among us has known it. It comforts the distressed, sweetens the heartbroken, soothes the troubled, scatters and destroys confusion. The soul, now separated from vice, and a stranger to carnal lust, is purged from sin. She knows that sweet and certain delight is awaiting her in the future, and so she is confirmed in hope, sure of attaining the Kingdom. And now, in her life here, she offers Christ a draught most delightful, warm with fervent love, laced with spiritual gifts, and adorned with the flowers of virtue. And Christ is pleased to accept it, for he, for the sake of love, *drank from the torrent on the way*.[1]

CHAPTER 30

The secret judgement of God on backsliders, who are not to be judged by us; a powerful attack on the money-makers.

BUT if someone should ask how it is that many of those who have lived the most austere lives, and seem completely to have given up worldly pleasure, are able to *return to their vomit again*[1] unafraid, and not attain their goal, we keep our peace and are silent, reluctant to pass judgement lest we should be wrong. It is not for us here to know God's hidden judgements: everything we need to know will be made clear in due course. All the ways of God are just and fair, fundamentally true and right, and he never rebukes this man independently of his wonderful justice, or that one without his great mercy, which is just too – and he does this in order that a man might choose life. So we ought to ponder the text, *the deep, like a garment, is his clothing*.[2]

1. cf. Psalms 110:7.   1. 2 Peter 2:22.   2. Psalms 104:6.

Chapter 30

We must be men who fear, then, while we are on the road, and never those who foolishly presume. No man knows whether he is worth hating or loving, or how he is going to finish when this life ends. Good people should fear lest they fall into evil, and evil men should hope to overcome their ill.

Moreover if men persist in their greed and wickedness, there is no point in their expecting to receive mercy before their sin has been dealt with. Sin is never forgiven before it is forsaken, and then only when satisfaction has been made by the sinner at the first opportunity.

But the worldly rich and powerful are consumed with an insatiable desire to get hold of other people's possessions, and by such wealth and goods to increase their own earthly greatness and worldly power, buying at small cost what is of great worth from the point of view of passing substance. They hold established positions in the service of kings or great men; they receive many gifts undeserved and unjustified; they get sensual delights and pleasures along with their honours. Let them hear the words, not of me, but of blessed Job: *They lead their lives in pleasure*, he says, *and they descend to hell in a moment*.[3] In a single moment they lose everything that throughout their life they had sought to acquire. With these people has dwelt *the wisdom of this world* which is called *foolishness with God*.[4] They have known the prudence of the flesh – and the enmity of God. And so the mighty suffer mighty torments, because *though they knew God, they did not glorify him as God*[5] but rather glorified themselves, and banished him from their thoughts. *Professing themselves to be wise, they became fools.*[6] And now those who had experienced the fame and delights of this life are come to the depths of stinking hell.

Indeed, of all those who have been bound up with the vices of this world, none, I reckon, have so little hope of salvation as those commonly called 'exploiters'.[7] For when they have spent all their youthful energy in getting hold of others' property by hook or crook, afterwards, in their old

3. Job 21:13.　　4. 1 Corinthians 1:18–25.　　5. Romans 1:21.
6. Romans 1:22.　　　　　　　　7. Latin *perpetratores*.

age, they sit back as if they were quite safe. Of course, they hang on to what they have wrongfully acquired. But conscience can be afraid, and their wickedness carries its own witness of condemnation. All they have done is merely to have ceased from their unjust exactions, for they do not hesitate to use others' property as if it were their own. Perhaps if they were to give it all back little would remain for themselves. But their pride will not allow them to beg, and they could not endure to fall from their erstwhile rank. *To dig*[8] they are unable. And so they choose, because demons have deceived them, to escape worldly woe in favour of suffering an eternal, endless hell!

Indeed, when such people lord it on earth they oppress lesser folk by their tyrannical power; and yet for others, the fact that they have not been exalted to such heights in their exile, is not a thing to be feared so much as to rejoice over; for lest the beloved of God should get like this, God restrains them, and they fulfil what the Psalmist says, *Be not afraid, though one be made rich, or if the glory of his house be increased.*[9] A man takes none of it with him when he dies, nor does his earthly splendour accompany him. There is not even a drop of water for the tongue of the rich man burning in hell.[10] He forfeits all his glory at death, and when he goes down into the shades only sin is his companion. For that he will be tormented in eternity.

CHAPTER 31

Why perfect contemplatives do not heed outward singing; the mistake of blaming them; the way of advance in contemplation.

BECAUSE there are in the church men and women duly appointed to sing the praise of God, and to stimulate people's devotion, folk have sometimes come and asked me why I do not want to do the same as the others, for they

8. Luke 16:3.　　　9. Psalms 49:16.　　　10. Luke 16:19-31.

have often seen me at Solemn Mass. They thought my attitude was wrong, for they said that all men ought to sing
aloud to their Creator, and give voice audibly. But I gave no
answer, because they knew neither the kind of music I
made for my Mediator, nor the sweet strains I bore. For
they fancied that no one could perceive spiritual song
because they themselves were unable to discover how it
could be. But it is stupid to think that one who wholly belongs to God may not receive a special gift from his Beloved, merely because they have had no such experience
themselves.

For this reason I thought I ought to show them some sort
of an answer, and not let those who argue in this way get
away with it. For what business is it of theirs the way other
people live, about whose manner of life they know nothing, whose life in many ways excels their own, and who
in the matter of 'things unseen' are much superior? Is God
not to be allowed to do what he wants? *Are their eyes evil
because he is good?*[1] Are they really wanting to cut the will
of God down to their size? Surely all men belong to God,
and he can take whom he wants, and leave whom he wills?
To whomsoever he wishes, whenever he chooses, he gives
whatever he pleases – and shows the magnificence of his
bounty!

I fancy the reason they grumble and grouse is that they
want those who are better than themselves to come down to
their level, and so conform to their inferiors. These people
think they are superior when in fact they are less! And so
my soul summoned up enough courage and I opened up to
them something of my music, which was springing from
the fire of love; that music in which I sing to Jesus, and
sound forth notes of sweetest harmony. But then they with-
stood me even more fiercely, because I sought to flee from
the 'outward' songs customarily sung in church, and from
the organ pieces that worshippers listen to: and because I
was only present when I needed to hear Mass – I could hear
it no other way – or when the importance of the day de-

1. Matthew 20:15.

141

manded it, to avoid arousing thereby the bitterness and backbiting of people!

Above all else I have always longed to sit and concentrate on Christ, and him alone. This was why he gave me spiritual song, by which I could offer praises and prayers to him. But those who argued with me did not share this opinion, and tried to make me conform to their pattern. But I could not possibly desert the grace of Christ, and accept the views of foolish men who were completely ignorant of all that was going on within me. I put up with all their talk, and I did what I had to do according to the state in which the Lord had placed me.

But I say all this, and give thanks and glory to Christ, so that now there need no longer be this sort of folly among people, this venturing to sit in judgement. What I have been doing has not been done in pretence or for fun, as some interpret my actions. Many indeed are led astray by such things, and believe themselves to have got what in fact is not theirs. But an unseen joy really has come to me, and in my soul I have been truly warmed with the fire of love.

It has lifted my heart above these lesser things, so that I now rejoice in Jesus, far away from outward melodies, but with one that is within.

In addition to my hatred of things that contaminate and my rejection of empty words, I have at the same time striven not to eat more food than necessary, nor to discipline myself stupidly – though I have been described as one who is addicted to rich men's houses, the pleasures of the table, and high living generally! But through the overruling of God I have had a soul differently ordered, which samples heavenly things rather than sweetmeats.

From that time I have never ceased to love solitude, and have chosen to live apart from men, as far as the needs of the body allow – and I have been continually upheld by him whom I love.

We must not be surprised if a man does not attain the heights of contemplation or experience its sweetness at the beginning of his Christian life. It is quite simple: to acquire contemplation means much time and hard work, and it is not given to anyone any time anyhow, even though its possession brings unspeakable joy. It is not within man's power to achieve it, and however great his efforts they will be inadequate. But God is generous, and it is granted to those who truly love him, and who have sought to love Christ beyond what men consider possible.

Yet many people after repentance fall away from their cleanness back into slackness and, indeed, into *the abomination of the Egyptians.*[2] Because they were not consumed with love their experience of the sweetness of contemplation was only occasional, and then but slight. And so, inadequate, they wilted under trial. Or perhaps it was that they became bored and scornful of God's *manna, and harked back to the fleshpots,*[3] wanting once again to live in worldly feasting and comfort.

If one is to despise the world, to desire the Kingdom, to hunger for the love of God, to hate sin, it is a great help to read or meditate regularly upon holy books. By these means the devout and instructed soul profits and develops, and has a ready defence against the darts of the enemy. The devil is confounded when we raise the word of God against his temptations. If indeed men can endure it, bearing *the burden and heat of the day*[4] patiently, never allowing themselves to be drawn into the love of false delights, after many tears and diligent prayers they will be inflamed with everlasting love, and feel within themselves a continual, unending warmth. For *while they are thus musing the fire kindled.*[5]

2. Deuteronomy 29:17.   3. Exodus 16:3.
4. Matthew 20:12.   5. Psalms 39:3.

CHAPTER 32

Instruction on the contemplative life, through prayer, medi-
tation, fasting, watching; false contemplatives and true; true
jubilant song.

THEREFORE an elect soul, completely absorbed in his
longing to love Christ, and Christ alone, transforms himself
into his Beloved. He has neither worldly possessions nor the
wish to possess any; in voluntary poverty he follows Christ,
and lives content on the alms of others. His conscience is
clear and sweet with heavenly savour, and he pours his
whole heart out in love for his Maker, striving every day to
grow in, and be consumed with, his longing for heaven. No
one who renounces this world in his zeal to be set alight on
fire by the Holy Spirit is going to allow his practice of
prayer and meditation to cool. For it is in this way, and by
the tears that result, and indeed by the favour of Christ
that the mind kindles in love most wonderfully, and
kindled rejoices, and rejoicing is raised to the life of contemplation. The soul which is in this excellent state flies up in
ecstasy; she is taken out of herself, and to her inner eye the
opened heaven offers its secrets for her gaze.

But first of all a man must exercise himself vigorously in
prayer and meditation for some years, virtually heedless of
his bodily needs. By his ardent use of these means, he rejects all that is unreal, and day and night eagerly seeks to
feel the love of God. In this way the almighty Lover inspires the one who loves him to fresh love, and raises him to
sublime heights, far above earthly things and the tumult of
vain and vicious thoughts. Now no *dead flies destroy the*
sweetness of the ointment,[1] for they have disappeared,
completely dead! And at last the love of God will become
sweet to him indeed, and he will be intoxicated with sweetness ever more rare; he will taste the honey of surpassing
wonder, so that in himself he knows only the comforting

1. Ecclesiastes 10: 1.

144

infusion of this heavenly savour, token of the highest sanctity. Anointed with sweetness of this sort he will strive to keep watching, for one who really feels his heart burn with the fire of eternal love is not going to let his mind turn away from this bright and sweet mystery. And yet some who were thought to be his equal had such fire only in their imagination. People like these, who are living, not in the truth but in the shades, when they are summoned to the Marriage Feast, think themselves fit to take the chief place. Not surprisingly at the true Judgement they will go down with *shame to find a lower place*.[2] For it is said of them, *A thousand shall fall at your side, and ten thousand at your right hand*.[3] If only they would try to know themselves, and search their own consciences! They would never then presume, or compare themselves with others' merits, and thus insult their betters!

The lover of the Godhead, whose whole being is shot through with love for the unseen Beauty, rejoices in the deep recesses of his soul; he is gladdened by that most delightful fire, for he has given himself to God with utter devotion. And so, not because he deserves it, but when Christ wills it, he will receive into his heart a sound sent from heaven; and then his meditation will be turned into melody, and his mind will dwell in marvellous harmony.

For it is angelic sweetness which he has received into his soul, and the songs of angels too, although his praise of God is not expressed in identical words. Yet his melody is similar to that of the angels, though again it is not as great or exact, for he is still hampered by corruptible flesh. He who has experienced this sweetness, has at the same time experienced the songs of angels, because they are both of one and the same kind: one here, the other in heaven. It is the tune that makes the song, not the words that are chanted. This praising is angelic food, not for the casual passer-by, but only for those who are most fervent in their love. They rejoice and delight in Jesus now that they have themselves been adjudged worthy to join in the eter-

2. Luke 14:9.   3. Psalms 91:7.

nal praise ever sung by the angels to God. The Psalmist sang of this, *Man has eaten angels' food.*[4] And so his nature is renewed, and will change into a divine glory and happiness. He will be sweet and godly and full of song because now he is feeling the delights of eternal love, singing unweariedly with the greatest sweetness. Then it is that there happens to such a lover what I have never found in any learned writing or have heard expounded, namely that this song will spring to his very lips, and he will sing his prayers in a spiritual symphony of celestial sweetness. It will make him slow of speech, because the abundance of his inner joy and the singular nature of his song impose delay, and what once occupied him not more than an hour he will now find difficult to complete in half a day. And while this is happening he will sit alone, mixing as little as possible with those who sing psalms, and deliberately not singing with the rest. I am not saying that all should try this, but let him to whom it is given do what he wishes, for he is being led by the Holy Spirit, and his way of life is not going to be diverted by what men say.

Moreover his heart will be living in splendour and fire, and marvellous music will exalt him. He will pay no particular respect to any one, even if he is thus thought to be an oaf or a bumpkin. In the depths of his being there is the praise of God and jubilant song, and his praise bursts out aloud; his most sweet voice rises up to heaven, and the Divine Majesty delights to hear it.

He whose beauty the King desires has a lovely face, because he holds within himself the uncreated wisdom. For his wisdom is drawn from the secret place, and her pleasures are for those who love eternity; she is not found by worldlings and their soft living. But she dwells in him of whom I have been speaking, because his whole being is absorbed in loving Christ, and all within him cries out for God. This cry is his love and his song, and he lifts a great shout to the ears of God. It is the longing of a good man, this eagerness for perfection. His is no worldly shout, for he

4 Psalms 78:25.

is craving Christ and none else. His inner being is ablaze
with the fire of love; his very heart is alight and burning; he
engages in no outward work which cannot be turned to
good. He praises God in song – but his song is in silence.
His lays are not meant for the ears of men; but in the sight
of God he utters his praise in unspeakable sweetness.

CHAPTER 33

*Spiritual song does not fit in with outward song; the reason
for the error of those who deny this; knowledge infused and
inspired, and how it differs from what has been acquired.*

A MAN raised to holiness can know that he has the song of
which I have been speaking in this way: he cannot abide
the noise of psalmody unless his own inner song is mentally
attuned to it; it is destroyed if he has to speak outwardly.
Some indeed are distracted in their singing and psalmody,
not because they are perfect, but because they are not yet
settled in their own minds, and people's words interrupt and
disturb their prayers; a thing which does not happen with
the perfect. For those who are well founded cannot be distracted from prayer or meditation by noise or tumult or
anything else: it is only from song that such things pluck
them. For that sweet, spiritual song is very special, and
given only to the most special! It is not an affair of those
outward cadences which are used in church and elsewhere;
nor does it blend much with those audible sounds made by
the human voice and heard by physical ears; but among
angel melodies it has its own acceptable harmony, and
those who have known it speak of it with wonder and
approval.

See and understand, you men, and do not be misled,
because I have shown you, for the honour of God Almighty
and our own blessing, why I used to escape these songsters,
and why I was not anxious to mix with them, or wanting to
hear organists play. As far as I am concerned they put an

obstacle in the way of sweet sound and oblige these splendid songs to cease. Do not be surprised then if I have fled from what would have been my undoing. I would have been at fault not to have left what I knew to be preventing me from this loveliest of songs. It would have been wrong to have acted otherwise. I know quite well from whom I received it, and I have striven to make myself do his will, lest he should take from graceless me what he had so graciously bestowed.

I used to delight indeed to sit alone, so that away from all the racket my song could flow more easily. With heartfelt fervour I would feel the sweetest joy, and undoubtedly I received this as a gift from him, him whom I have loved above all things and beyond description.

For it is not as though my heart has been seething with bodily lust, nor was it from any creature that I got these consoling songs which I delight to sing to Jesus. It is love that has been poured into me, not that I should live depressed like some outcast, but rather that I should be lifted up beyond the most exalted of things visible, and aflame and radiant, praise God from heaven: his praise is not seemly from a foul mouth!

Therefore it is to him that the window will be opened, that window which is opaque to all those who love any but the one thing needful. Not surprisingly such a man's nature is transformed into a nobility of immeasurable worth, free and splendid. This noble freedom they shall never know who know neither the love nor the sweetness which is in Christ here on earth.

Quite obviously I must not stop my devotion which has now been so thoroughly tested just because some detractors have been snarling maliciously against my innocence. Indeed I must fight all wickedness, and still love those who stir up even greater trouble for me. For grace will increase for the lover all the while he heeds not windy words, but reaches out with perfect heart to his Beloved, tireless in the pursuit of his purpose.

And so his love of vanity vanishes, for true love is unfolding in his mind, for to him who loves there is no cooling down of soul, but a persistent strengthening of warmth, and a heart unwavering in its continual meditation on the Beloved. In this steadfastness, indeed, the true lover experiences the excellence of love, for it means that he will be taken up into the fiery heaven, and there set ablaze with unspeakable love, his whole being inwardly on fire more fully than can be expressed. There he will make his own the degrees of grace from which have come his wisdom and insight, so that now he knows how to speak among the wise, and to state boldly what he thinks needs saying, even though hitherto people have taken him for a fool and simpleton – as perhaps he was.

But those who have acquired their learning not directly but second-hand, and who are puffed up with their complicated arguments, say scornfully, 'Where did he learn all this? To which teacher has he been listening?' They do not believe that lovers of eternity can be taught by an inner Teacher, or speak more eloquently than those taught by men who have spent their whole life studying for empty honours.

But if the Holy Spirit inspired many people in days gone by, why should he not raise his lovers to contemplate the glory of God today? For some of our contemporaries are approved as being the equals of those of the past. Yet I am not calling what is only an opinion of men 'approval', because men are often wrong in what they approve, for they choose people that God has rejected, and reject those whom he has chosen. But those are 'approved' whom the love of eternity inflames through and through, whom the grace of the Holy Spirit inspires to all good. These are marked out because they are adorned with every kind of virtue; because they always rejoice in God's love; and because everything that belongs to vain and worldly pleasure, to the sham honours and the detestable pride of life, their affections tread underfoot. No doubt they are rejected by men – but in the sight of God and his holy angels they are thought magnificent. Their hearts are resolute to endure all opposition, nor will they let themselves be blown about by the wind of vanity. And in the end they are carried up to Christ, in sublime holiness, while those who were chosen and 'approved' by men are cast out into damnation, dragged into torment, and punished with the fiends for ever.

CHAPTER 34

The supreme excellence of jubilant song; it cannot be told or recorded; it has no peer; the love of those who sing, and the pride of those who have acquired knowledge.

IT is both understandable and right that the lover of God should be caught up to gaze mentally on things above, and to sing of the love that surges through his soul. There the fire of love blazes fierce and bright, filling him with sweet devotion. His whole being is a hymn, beautiful and fragrant with his Redeemer's sweetness. And as he sings he is led on to utter delight; and with the inner fount of fervour welling up he is taken into the sweet, warm caress of God. The lover is overwhelmed and enriched with the most intense ardour through this unique consolation, and carried on his glorious way. He shines whiter than snow, and glows redder than any rose, for he is alight with God's fire. Arrayed with a clean conscience, he walks in white. He has been taken up, almost as it were in secret, above all others because of the melody that is ever in his heart, and the sweet, persisting richness of his fervour. And not only does he offer in his own person a wholehearted sacrifice as he praises Christ in spiritual music, but he also encourages others to love, so that they hurry to give themselves wholly and devoutly to God. And this, to anyone who loves him and cleaves to him with all his heart, brings joy in their exile. For the delightful taste that the love of Jesus has brought him exceeds the bounds of experience, and I am not adequate to describe even slightly the smallest part of this joy. For who can describe ineffable fervour? Who lay bare infinite sweetness? Certainly if I were wanting to speak about this inexpressible joy I would seem to be trying to empty the sea drop by drop, and bit by bit to squeeze it all into a tiny hole in the earth!

Little wonder that I who have scarcely tasted a drop of that excellence am quite unable to find words to tell of the immensity of such eternal sweetness! Small wonder, too, that you with your dulled sensitivity and distracting carnal thoughts are incapable of receiving it, even though you might be wise and clever and always about God's business.

Yet if you really sought to acquire a taste for heavenly things, and studied to be kindled with love for God, there can be no doubt that the same delightful sweetness would flow abundantly into you, and impart its wonderful pleasure wherever it could find a place in your soul. The fuller you are of charity, the greater your capacity, you may reckon, for that joy. Certainly in eternity those will stand closer to God who have loved him more fervently and sweetly here. But they who have no love for God whatever are full of earthly corruption, and so they cling to empty fairy-tales, and look for satisfaction in the enjoyment of outward and visible possessions. They know nothing of those inner blessings whose upward reach is hidden from mortal eyes. Because they wholeheartedly give themselves over to passing comforts, in their pride they lose sight of any glorious future!

In the life to come it is clear that it will be greed that will be exiled, and charity that will reign – contrary to what is held by many today, indeed by nearly everyone. For greed has found its way even into the royal court, and charity, as if it were some sort of traitor, is imprisoned, or banished from the realm. Yet it finds a home in the hearts of the elect. It turns away from the proud; it stays with the humble.

Many pitiful creatures are deceived, thinking they are loving God when they are not. They imagine they can engage in worldly business, and at the same time really enjoy the love of Jesus Christ and his sweetness. They believe they can rush about the world and still be contemplatives – something which those who love God fervently and who have entered the contemplative life know to be impossible. But they in their folly and lack of heavenly wisdom, are puffed up with such knowledge as they have acquired, and have a wrong idea of themselves. They do not yet know how to hold on to God with love.

So I look up with longing and cry, *'Save me, God, for your saint is weak.'*[1] The hymn-singing fails, the voice of the songsters falls silent, the fervour of saintly lovers is missing. Everyone is going about his own evil way; the deceit each has conceived in his heart is not prevented from bearing fruit. *They spend their days with vanity, and their years with haste.*[2] Alas, the fire of lust has swallowed up youth and maid alike, baby and old man.

Good Jesus, how good it is to cleave to you!
For my soul will not come into their counsels,[3]
   but I will sit in solitude, and sing to you in my joy.
Your sweetness increases with praising,
   so to praise you continually is no hard matter, but
      rather sweet;
   no bitter thing, but something more pleasant by far
   than any amount of physical and worldly delight.
It is at once delightful and desirable to live and praise
      you,
   for all that exists has been fashioned with such love,
   and is redolent of such fragrance
   – and who can wonder at it?

Once he has been purged of his obscenities and all those thoughts which are not directed to this one thing, the lover, ablaze through these same spiritual caresses, strains with all his might to gaze upon his Beloved. And his shout, excited and bursting out from the core of his longing love, goes up, of course, to his Maker, though to him it seems as if he were shouting from far off. He lifts up that inner voice, which only exists in those who love most fervently, to the utmost of his power...

1. Psalms 12:1.   2. Psalms 78:33.   3. cf. Psalms 1:1.

But here I have to 'give up' because of my inherent stupidity and dullness; I have not the wit to describe this shout or its magnitude, or even the pleasure it gives just to think of it, or feel it, or experience it. Neither now nor in the future will I be able to tell you, because I do not know how to overcome the limitations of my senses; all I want to say is that the shout is the song.

Then where is one who will sing me the music of my songs, the joys of my longing, the fervour of my love, the warmth of my youthful yearning, so that from this fellow-ship of love and song I might at least search out my inmost being? So that the measure of music for which I was thought worthy might be made known to me? So that I might find myself freed from unhappiness? What I cannot claim for myself, because I have not found what I hope for so eagerly, I might be able to enjoy in the sweet comfort of my friend.

If indeed I thought that that shout and song were always hidden from outward ears – which is actually what I am venturing to say – what would I give to find a man who was experienced in that melody? Having recorded that which was unspoken he could sing to me my joy, and produce those flowing notes and songs which in the Name above all others I have not been ashamed to set before my Beloved. I would love such a one above gold, and none of the precious things we have here in our exile would I deem his equal. For the beauty of virtue would dwell with him, and he would in truth search out the mysteries of love. In short, I would love him as I love my heart, nor would I dream of hiding anything from him. He would reveal to me the song I long to understand, and he would make plain and clear my joyous shout. The more I understood, the fuller would be my exultation, and surely the more fruitful my emula-tion of him. The fire of love would be shown me, and my joy and song would shine out for all to see. My confused thoughts would then lack no one to put them into praise, nor would I toil to no purpose.

Yet now the fatigues of this deplorable exile press heavily

upon me, and their burdens aggravate and nearly kill me. And though within I am glowing with uncreated warmth, outwardly I appear depressed, skulking in misery, with no light at all!

So, my God, to whom I offer my heartfelt devotion, will you not remember me in your mercy? I am wretched, and I need your mercy. Will you not bring up into your light the longing which so grips me, that in your own good time I may have what I crave? The toil by which I atone for my sin, you will transform into a dwelling of great sweetness, so that where sadness has dwelt melody may now live, and I see in the splendour of his beauty my Beloved and my Desire. Held in his clasp I would praise him for ever, for after him I long.

CHAPTER 35

The meditation of one who longs for his Beloved, and his lack of any companion; the orderly progress of him who comes to the fire of love.

Jesus, when I am in you, and on fire with joy,
  and when the heat of love is surging in,
  I want to embrace you, the most loving, with my whole
    being.
Yet, my Beloved, I am held back from what I long for.
And, too, there are difficulties to be met,
  for a vast wilderness bars the way
  to stop the lovers' homes from being united.

If only you would send me a companion for my journey
  so that the longing could be lightened by his
    encouragement,
  and the chain of my sighings loosed!
For if that lovely vision of yourself
  does not come quickly and release me,
  it will press so heavily on your lover
  as to force him to leave this prison of flesh,

and by reason of the very greatness of his love
to throw himself down before your Majesty!
In the meantime I would indeed rejoice to hymn you,
and live in happiness with the one you had given me
with much positive and honest talk.
Our very eating, to be sure, would be enjoyed in love,
and in turn we would pour out our loving lays,
until we were released from our visible prison,
brought into our invisible home,
and allotted a place among heaven's folk,
who have loved Christ even as we have.

But, alas, what am I to do? How long have I to wait? To
whom shall I flee to enjoy what I am longing for? For I am
needy and famished, tortured and afflicted, wounded and
wan because my Love is not here; for this immense love
torments me, and the hope deferred afflicts my soul. And so
the cry of my heart goes up, and in the midst of the
heavenly choir there moves my music and my musing,
eager to be raised to audience with the Most High. And
when it gets there it proclaims its business, and says

'My love, my honey, my harp,
my psalter and song the whole day long!
When are you going to heal my grief?
You, the root of my heart,
when are you coming to receive my spirit
which is always looking for you?
I am wounded to the quick by your fair beauty.
My longing knows no respite,
but builds up more and more.
My present afflictions pierce and oppress me,
so I hasten to you,
for from you only can I hope for solace and healing.
But who meanwhile will show me
the end of my trials and troubles?
And who is going to tell me
about the fullness of my joy,
and the fulfilling of my song,

so that I get comfort from these things,
and rejoice in my happiness?
And this, moreover, so that I might know
that my own perfecting
and the finish of my misery was at hand?'

Then would I burst out with splendid song, and maybe my voice would soften the severity of my Beloved did he want to chastise me, or strike me down. He would not mock the innocent's pain, as little by little he punished him.

And henceforth I could be called happy, and enjoy the eternal, delightful refreshment of love, freed from all uncleanness. And rid of grief I would live in perfect holiness, pouring out my joyful praise in harmony with the heavenly symphony – even as I try to do now in my poverty and hardship.

The warmth of this sweet-sounding love rejoices my inmost being; the sweet, deep recollection of Jesus entrances my mind as it were with music, and much cheered by this heavenly song I feel nothing of the sweet poison of those worthless delights which they who flourish in the flesh find so attractive. No troublesome earthiness will get hold of me!

You who are the most lovely,
lovable, and beautiful,
remember that it is through you
that I am no longer afraid of any passing power;
and remember, too, that in order to cling closely to you
I have rejected the love
which seduces fools from loving you, my God.
Remember how quickly I fled those fleeting beauties
which captivate men,
and make women, poor things, so wicked.
I have never wanted to indulge
in those youthful, unclean follies
which subject souls freeborn to such foolish servitude.
More, I have never ceased to show you my heart
stricken with longing for yourself.

And you have kept it safe,
   lest it should drain away into lustful wastes,
   and you have implanted it
   with the remembrance of your Name,
   and have opened to its eye
   the window of contemplation.
And now at last I have run to you
   with my song and devotion.
But not before my heart had kindled
   with the fire of love,
   and deep within me I had burst into songs of love.
And since these things are ever in your sight
   your boundless mercy reminds you
   not to leave your lovers in the cold too long,
   and so I believe you will ease my misery,
   and not turn your face from my longing.
Pain and misery are ever the lot of the body;
   but my soul persists in its longing
   until you give me what I have been wanting so intensely.
Because of this love my flesh has withered
   and become of little worth,
   in the midst of so much that is attractive in this life.
And in the same way my soul has languished
   until she see you,
   for she has been wanting you so vehemently,
   longing to be seated in deepest heaven,
   and to rest in the fellowship so much desired,
   taken up where the angels sing,
   to enjoy you in perfection and for ever.
See, my inmost being is in ferment,
   and the flame of charity
   has consumed the hateful confusion of my heart,
   and eliminated the slimy happiness of unclean friend-
     ships,
   and wiped out the stupid thoughts
   which were so odious when one honestly looked at them.
I have genuinely attained a real love,
   I who once was asleep in my varied and devious errors,

enveloped in spiritual darkness.
And I have felt the delight of devotion sweetest
where now I most grieve that I once failed.

Listen to me, friends, I beg you lest you be led astray too! These words, and words which in the sight of our Creator are like them, flare up from my love. No one strange to this vast love should dare to handle such things, nor he who is disturbed by tempting, vain, and useless thoughts, nor he whose mind is not surely set on Christ, nor he who loves created things, whose heart does not go wholly out to God, because it feels itself bound by some earthly affection.

On the other hand he is supreme in charity whose heart has sung the love-songs of devotion. Preserved and nourished spiritually, he has no time for outward follies. Indeed, he is wonderfully cheered by these everlasting delights, and by them raises himself to contemplate heavenly things. There he glows with sweetest love, his thirst slaked on his heavenly way by most delightful refreshment. The radiance of his coming happiness is already surrounding and transforming him, so that he eschews all temptation, set as he is on the pinnacle of the contemplative life. And thereafter he triumphs in constant song to the praise of Christ.

CHAPTER 36

The different gifts of the elect; how the saints progressed towards love, by prayer, meditation, loving, enduring hardship, and by hating vice; love comes from God; remembrance of him by the lover is needful; the lover does not fall into carnal temptations as do the imperfect; he is not hurt by the spark of sin, though it persists.

THE chosen of God who have loved him beyond all measure, and whose minds are set on loving him more than anything else, show us in a remarkable way the secret of such love, for they have welcomed the fire of love with a fervour that is above telling and beyond nature, yearning for their beloved Jesus with indescribable affection. For the lovers of God are endowed with a variety of gifts; some are chosen for action, some for teaching, some for loving. Yet all his saints care for this one thing, and hasten in the same direction, though by different paths. For in the providence of God each one goes on to the Kingdom by way of that virtue to which he is most accustomed. And if the virtue he excels in draws him to cleave more fervently to the sweetness of God's love – it is reckoned to be stronger where there is the greatest peace – assuredly he will come to God, and receive for his prize that eternal, glorious mansion and throne which has been ordained by Christ to be the everlasting possession of those who love most perfectly.

Those lovers who used to sing the glorious songs of love were accustomed to say that he who is chosen primarily to love cares above all that his heart shall never depart from his Beloved, and that the recollection of Jesus may be as music at a feast, sweeter to the taste than honey and the honeycomb.[1] And the longer he exercises himself in spiritual studies the sweeter does Jesus seem. So then he withdraws his mind from silly and sinful thoughts and puts it to wanting his Creator. Everything he brings into Christ to set it in him, the fount of love. To love him only, and find joy in him alone, is his unceasing prayer.

And now there come into his soul sweet desires and wonderful meditations directed to God alone. When he has brooded on them, and given his mind to develop them, they have an unutterable effect on him, and with great delight and spiritual sweetness lead him on to the contemplation of heavenly things, purging his mind from the hunger for worldly comfort. At this time the lover of God wants nothing so much as to be alone, to attend only to the wishes of his Maker. And when he has been well exercised in all this, and is given over to prayer and meditation in great quiet, and when all wickedness and uncleanness have been destroyed, and he takes up his arduous journey with prudence, he will make wonderful progress in the virtue of

1. cf. Ecclesiasticus 49:1.

eternal love. His desires rise even higher, and with the eyes of his soul he enters into, and sees, the mysteries of heaven.

A fire which his soul had not felt previously now begins to inflame him, and while he is absorbed in these lovely things, begins to warm him, now more intensely, now less so, to the limit permitted the soul by her corruptible body, with its many burdens and troubles.[2] So the soul, anointed with the sweetness of heaven, and breathing its soft air, longs to set out heavenward, but feels frustrated because she must remain in this mortal flesh. Nonetheless she gladly endures whatever adversity comes her way, for she is resting sweetly in the joy of eternal love. Nothing can take away her happiness and her gladness in Jesus. Indeed the schemings of the devil stop, reduced to impotence, and the deceitful vanity of worldly honour is despised, and the enervating appeal of the flesh is neither looked for nor wanted. And it is these things that are the weapons they use against God's chosen ones, if that by using them without warning and all together at once they might stampede them into wrong – those who live in heaven![3]

But they are powerless and rejected, because the holy lover of God in the name of the resolute Christ says, simply and joyfully, '*You are my defender*,'[4] so that those who oppose me, my enemies who attack me maliciously, do not disturb my peace. But *you*, too, *are my glory*, because I glory in you, not in my own strength, which would not exist if it did not come from you. Rightly indeed is everything referred to you, and nothing to me, for *you lift up my head*, that higher part of my soul, by which with your permission the lower parts are ruled. And you raise my soul to song and to the contemplation of heavenly things, and will not allow her to be cast down into those lower, vile pleasures of the world, or to get involved in them. This is what *head* means, because you have so increased it with the oil of spiritual gladness that it is now enlarged with charity. And *my cup overflows*[5] signifies a draught of inner sweet-

2. cf. Wisdom 9:15.   3. cf. Philippians 3:20.
4. Psalms 3:3.   5. Psalms 23:5.

ness, intoxicating my soul with love for my Maker, so that I rest secure, the love of passing things completely put behind me. And so with a sort of sweetness I am led on to glorious eternity, feeling neither earthly pleasure nor distress.'

For in this incomparable, loving sweetness our conscience becomes radiant, for there purity is lasting, and the heart grows delightfully warm. And the mind, amazed at all these gifts, gets more fervent; she does not pause to consider the attractions of our exile here, but embraces more gladly the bitter things of earth rather than the sweet. She is enjoying imperishable delights, and not for a single moment does she cease to cling to the love of Jesus. Her desire is so ardent that you might sooner and more easily turn the world upside down than call her mind away from the love of her Saviour.

She hates everything that is contrary to the love of God, and in her fervour is tireless in doing the things which she sees and knows will please him. Nor will she give this up for whatever pain or grief that seeks to hinder. Quite the reverse: it means that she hastens more earnestly than ever to do the will of God, if for his sake she can find some hardship to endure. She neither thinks nor wants anything save truly to love Christ, and in all things always to do whatever pleases him.

She has got this fiery will from her Beloved through the bounty of God, her mind rich with godly devotion indeed. For he chose her to be such, that she might ever be Christ's perfect lover; that she might be made a vessel of his choosing, filled with the most noble wine of a sweet and heavenly life; that his Name, chosen from the thousands that are, might continue an undying, everlasting memorial, kept ever by her in her inmost heart. By the help of God she will reject everything that hinders love, and will delight wholly in him. The darts of the enemy will not prevail against lovers of this sort.

But she will receive from her Beloved the blessed assurance and the indescribable radiance of her inner sweetness as moment by moment she surrenders her spirit to him. Because there is deep down within her this crying after him, each day she is renewed by her burning, loving devotion, so that nothing that is spiritually foul or corrupt can live in her. All the while her thought continues to be God-directed every wicked suggestion put up by the malice of the enemy is rejected. The fire of love really does dwell in her mind, and it purges every sinful infection that unregenerate lust would put in her way.

And now, set in truth on the topmost height, the affection is so sure of itself that it is always on the look-out for the least carelessness, to cast it away as if it too were a pestilential enemy. While it lives it never lets go its vigilance and fear. For the better a man is, and the more acceptable to God, so much the more does he burn with charity. And so he is stirred by the same prompting of love to perform with ever greater urgency and vigour those things which are compatible with his state and life. Thus he is always keen not to lose even for a single moment the recollection of his Beloved and Sweetest, so that not only in theory but in fact he may possess him and think of him whom he knows he is bidden to love with all his heart. He is terribly afraid of being drawn into even the smallest things that offend him. For not only does he strain to fulfil what he has been bidden to do, to love Christ with all his mind – and he strives with all his longing! – but he is also seized with a great delight, so that he never forgets his Beloved, nor wants to be separated from his love by inclining to passing delights, even if it were possible for him to do what he wanted without penalty. He knows by experience that spiritual pleasures are sweeter than physical loves. It would be very surprising if he lapsed into such absurdity; if by spurning his spiritual gifts he prepared to enjoy what was false and fantastic; or if he chose to get engrossed in that carnal beauty hated by every saintly lover of God.

It is not surprising, however, that the 'lust of the flesh' has deceived some in its evil way. Beauty paraded and exposed has been known to draw even the wise and devout into her

illicit embrace. But this can only happen if they are not
perfectly grounded in charity, or really cleaving to eternal
love. So when they are attacked by temptation, though they
have seemed to be making progress, before they reach the
summit they collapse in ruins.

But there can be no doubt that the true lover of the
everlasting never loses his peace in the midst of temptations. He gains his crown in this warfare, while others less
stable are slain. The beloved of Christ never fail to cut
down whatever stands in their way, even while they are
pouring out their hearts to their Maker. They are not in the
least like those who in the highway of love are unsteady on
their feet, and who if they are cast down from their intended ascent just give up. They for their part prepare for
eternal joys without faltering, and go unshakable from the
first. Nourished and taught as they are by the sweetness of
heaven's savour, they brighten those outside by the example of their sanctity, and among themselves they burn
sweetly with the fire of love. The errors of carnal affection
they will mortify by their passion for purity, though no one
in this life can wholly quench unregenerate lust, or be so
perfect as to live in the flesh without sinning. It is not in
this life, through this means or that, that a man is healed
and made perfect, but only in the fatherland. There glory
strengthens his capacity to behold God, and everlasting
peace conquers grief and pain. No corruption remains to
worry over when eternal bliss crowns the triumph!

Meanwhile the mind remains alert, longing to keep its
fire of love constant, and striving to escape the pleasures of
visible vanity. And it will persist in this purpose until death.
But in death both the urge to sin and the natural longing
perish. So each elect soul will seek to develop his love, and
strengthened and armed against this sinful urge by heavenly
grace and self-control, will throw himself into the glorious
struggle, and fight to the end against everything opposed
to the lovers of God.

Hence it happens that while the fighter is overcoming –
and is not being overcome – he is elated with a wonderful

joy, which delights his whole being. He knows himself inspired by this mysterious love, and in its sweet warmth rises higher still, to contemplate with joy and to pour out sweet praise upon his Lover. Meantime his carnal urges hasten to their death and to complete extinction.

Some would add to this and say that there sounds in their heart something sweet and tuneful, by which the thirsty soul is ravished and gladdened. But they do not explain, as far as I can make out, how it is that their thought is changed into song, or how the melody remains in the mind, or with what joy it is that he sings his prayers.

CHAPTER 37

The true lover loves only his Beloved; two kinds of rapture; outside the body, and by raising the mind to God; the excellence of this second way.

THE fervour of the spirit whose longing is stimulated by the beauty of God, displays a pure love: he wants nothing but his Beloved, and every other affection has been completely extinguished. So now his mind is freely borne to his sweet love, and the bond between their two wills is strengthened and made firm. Nothing is able now to hinder the lover from his purpose, or to make him have second thoughts, so that, loving and supremely happy, he can at last achieve his desire, and with every obstacle gone, run as fast as he can into his Love's arms.

Among all the delights he is enjoying, he is now aware of a heavenly secret infused into his sweet love, and known only by himself. And he has about him that honeyed balm which so thrills the joyful lovers of Jesus and makes them in their happiness hurry ever faster to those heavenly seats where they are to enjoy the glory of their Creator for ever. Even as they gaze at the things of heaven they are pining for this. On fire within, their inmost being rejoices to be illumined with such delightful splendours. It feels as if they are being carried away with most pleasurable love, absorbed in wonderful joy and song.

In this way their thinking is made sweet as they serve him, because whether studying, or meditating on Scripture, or writing, or expounding, their thoughts are continually with their Beloved, yet it never lessens their normal measure of praise. What indeed might be thought remarkable is the fact that one mind can perform two things at once, and attend to each at one and the same time; when, for example, it offers and sings its loving praises to Jesus, mentally rejoicing, and while this is going on, can understand what is written in books – and neither conflicts with the other!

But this grace is not granted to all and sundry, but only to the holy soul filled with the utmost holiness, in whom shines love in all its splendour, and in whom hymns of love, inspired by Christ, spontaneously arise. She becomes, so to speak, an instrument of praise in the sight of her Maker, vibrant with unspeakable joy. The soul knows now the mystery of love, and rises up with a great shout and intense delight to her Beloved. Her insight is most acute, her awareness most sensitive; it is not dissipated in this worldly thing or that, but everything is integrated and secured in God, whom she serves with her pure conscience, and her splendid mind; her God whom she is pledged to love, and to whom surrender.

The purer the love of the lover, the closer is God's presence to him; the purer his rejoicing in God, the more abundant his experience of God's goodness, kindness, and sweetness. For God likes to infuse these very things into all who love him, and quietly to enter godly hearts to their incomparable delight. Love is truly pure when it is not diluted with a wish for anything else, however little; when there is not the least inclination to seek pleasure in the enjoyment of physical beauty. For the lover finds that his mind, already keen, is made clean as well, and completely fixed in its overruling passion for eternity. Free in the Spirit, he looks ever at *the things that are above*[1] with the in-

1. Colossians 3: 1.

tensity of one rapt away from the beauty of all other things, to which he will not turn, and which he cannot love.

It is clear that 'enraptured' can be understood in two ways. One way is when a man is rapt out of all physical sensation, so that at the time of his rapture his body quite clearly feels nothing and does nothing. He is not dead, of course, but alive, because his soul is still vitalizing his body. Sometimes the saints and the elect have been enraptured in this fashion, for their own good, and for others' enlightenment. Thus Paul was rapt to the *third heaven*.[2] Even sinners sometimes experience raptures of this sort in visions, and see the joy of the good, or the punishment of the wicked; this is for their correction or for that of others. We have read this of many.

But 'rapture' in the other sense comes through the lifting up of the mind to God in contemplation; all perfect lovers of God go this way – and only those who love God. It is as accurate to call this 'rapture' as the other, because there is a definite seizure, a something outside nature. For surely it is supernatural that out of some vile sinner can be made a child of God, full of spiritual joy and borne up to God. This second way is most desirable and lovely. For Christ was always contemplating God, yet it never detracted from his self-possession.

So one way is to be rapt by love while retaining physical sensation, and the other is to be rapt out of the senses by some vision, terrifying or soothing. I think that the rapture of love is better, and more rewarding. For to have the privilege of seeing heavenly things is a matter of God's gift, not our merit.

'Rapt', too, can be used of those who are wholly and perfectly subservient to their Saviour's wishes; they deservedly rise up to the heights of contemplation. Their illumination is that of God's uncreated wisdom, and their desert is to feel the heat of that indescribable light with whose beauty they are enraptured.

This also happens when a devout soul has every thought

2. 2 Corinthians 12:2.

controlled by her love for God; when all the waywardness
of her mind has been settled, and she no longer wavers or
hesitates; when all her love has led to one thing, and with
great ardour she yearns for Christ, reaching out to him
and meaning him – for all the world as if there only existed
these two, Christ and her loving soul. Bound indissolubly to
him in love and in ecstasy of mind, she is off and away,
surmounting every physical barrier to drink deep from the
chalice of heaven, which is wonderful beyond belief. She
could never have attained this had not the grace of God
rapt her from her weak desires, and planted her on the
spiritual heights where, not surprisingly, she receives the
gifts of grace.

So when she consciously considers only those things that
are divine and heavenly, with a heart now free and unshakable she finds her mind swept away and rapt to heaven, far
above all material, visible things. Now she is genuinely on
the point of receiving and feeling in herself the heat of love,
and is about to dissolve into a song of honeyed sweetness.
For this is the consequence when one is rapt and chosen.
This is why rapture is such a great and marvellous thing,
and, as it seems to me, superior to everything else we do in
life: it is reckoned to be the certain foretaste of everlasting
sweetness. It surpasses, unless I am mistaken, all other gifts
in this earthly pilgrimage which God bestows on the saints
by way of reward. In some respect they deserve their higher
place in heaven, because in this life they have loved God
with greater ardour and quietness. (The greatest quiet is
necessary to procure and preserve such love, because if
there is too much movement, unsettlement, or mental in-
stability, it cannot be received or retained.) Therefore when
one is chosen and raised up for this he lives full of great joy
and virtue and he dies in sweet assurance. After this life he
will be even more glorious, even nearer to God, in the midst
of choirs of angels.

Meanwhile he has this delight, warmth, and song which I
touched on at some length earlier, and through them he
serves God, and loving God he clings close to him, so as

never to be parted. But since this corruptible body bears heavily on the soul, and our earthly dwelling hinders the mind in its much thinking, he cannot always rejoice with the same ease, nor does he always sing with the same clarity and consistency. For sometimes his soul feels warmth and sweetness to be stronger, and then she finds it difficult to sing. Sometimes indeed when she would sing she is rapt with wonderful sweetness and fluency; yet when the warmth is felt to be less she will often fly off into song with the greatest pleasure, and, in ecstasy, she knows that the heat and sweetness are with her in truth. Yet there is never heat without delight, though sometimes it can be without song, for physical singing or noise can hinder it and drive it back into thought.

But in the solitude they meet more openly, for there the Beloved speaks to the heart. It is very much like the bashful lover who will not embrace his girl in public, or even greet her as a friend, but behaves as though she is like anybody else – even as if she were a stranger!

The devout soul who has definitely put away all distracting things, and whose heartfelt desire is only to enjoy the delights of Christ, and who yearns fervently for him, comes soon to the loveliest joy. Melody pours out from him, bringing wonderful pleasure to his soul, which she takes as a sign that from now on she will not be able normally to endure any worldly sound. For this music is spiritual music, unknown to those who are taken up with worldly affairs, lawful or otherwise. And no one has ever known it but he who has striven to have time only for God.

CHAPTER 38

The desire of the lover for God is explained; the love of the world is shown to be detestable by many examples; the remembrance of God does not last long in those who love the world.

No one can untie the knot
  by which I bind your love to me, sweet Jesus.
I am seeking the treasure I long for,
  but all I can find is longing,
  because I never stop thirsting for you!
Yet like the wind my sorrow vanishes,
  for my reward is this melody inaudible to human ear.
My inner being is turned into a song wonderfully sweet,
  and because of this love I want to die.
Whenever this occurs, and these things
  take hold of me and refresh me,
  then the size of your gifts dazzles and delights me,
  and love's approach tortures me with joy.

But still I lack those things which show the Beloved to the one who longs for him. And this wounds me, and fills me with longing, but gives no ease at all; rather it increases it, because with my growing love my longing increases too. *My life is spent with sorrow, and my years with sighing*[1] because I am parted from my Beloved, because my desire to die is not satisfied, because the remedy for my wretchedness is still not here. I rise up and cry, *Woe to me that my exile is prolonged.*[2] Love it is that tortures me, love that delights me. It tortures, because what is loved so much is not immediately granted me; yet it delights, because it refreshes me with hope, and infuses indescribable comfort through its very heat.

For a mighty longing develops when there is in the soul through its joy and love the song of songs, and the fierce

1. Psalms 31:10. 2. Psalms 120:5.

heat produces further sweet delight. For now one likes to think that death is life. For the flower that this thought nourishes can never die, but the splendour which all the while is growing in the lover, and which seems so wonderful, makes of death and music one thing. For when I come to die the fullness of my beatitude which the Almighty, my love, is going to grant me will begin. To be sure, my seat is made ready in that place where love knows no cooling off, no fading into inertia. For his love kindles my heart, because I can already feel his fire; there is no pressure on my spiritual strength while I am wholly held within the consolation of such love.

Nonetheless I faint because of love, and spend all my time in holy sighing. Nor will this be to my disadvantage with the angels of God, for whose fellowship I so ardently yearn, and with whom I too firmly hope and expect to be perfected. On the other hand, joyful praise will cheer the longing one, and the Beatific Vision, so dear and so loved, will reveal itself openly.

But woe indeed to those who have wasted and spent their days in vanity, whose years have swiftly perished with no fruit of charity to show. They long with a love that is unclean for the decadent beauty of the flesh, which is but the cloak for decay and corruption, and leads to a joyless death. On them also a fire has fallen, the fire of greed and wrath, and they will not see the sun of everlasting light. These will go off into the Beyond, still following after vanity; vain like the things they loved. Then, when they are judged, they will see a fierce Christ, and in their eyes intolerable, because in this life they never felt him sweet to their hearts.

But those who do feel in themselves that he is delightful here, undoubtedly will see him in all his attractiveness there. For what he is to us now, such he will appear to us then; to the lover, lovable and desirable; to the non-lover, hateful and cruel. And the difference will not be in him, but in us. He himself is unchangeably the same, but every creature will see him according to his deserts. For he shows himself voluntarily to each man as he wills. So that at one and the same time he will appear pleased to the righteous, and angry to the unrighteous.

The love of a rational soul behaves in that way, good or bad, according to which it shall be judged. There is nothing more effective for gaining the joy of eternity than the love of Christ, nor for bringing about utter damnation than the love of the world. So let eternal love inflame our minds, and the wild and hateful love of carnal affections be thrown out. Let the sweetness of the heavenly life so intoxicate us that we just do not want to like life's bitter sweetness here, because the *poison of dragons*[3] (the basest wickedness and lying bitterness) is the *wine of the ungodly*. Drinking it they are made so drunk that they give no heed to what their future will be. And the *venom of asps* (murderous evil) is deadly drink to them: there is no cure for them, for their wickedness is incorrigible.

True, this lying world has its delights of miseries, its riches of vanities, its hurtful charms, its pestilential pleasures, its sham happiness, its insane love; its mindless, hateful affection, the darkness of its high noon which ends in eternal night. It too has its savourless salt, its flat flavours, its twisted honour, its horrible friendliness (so sweet in the morning, so revolting at night), its bitter honey, its deadly fruit. It too has its rose that stinks, its joy that weeps, its melody of sadness, its approval of contempt, its really deadly nectar, its attractive abominations, its misleading leader, its domineering prince. And it has its lamentable jewellery, and its sneering praise, its black lily, its rackety song, its decadent beauty, its discordant harmony, its soiled snow, its cheerless comfort, its poverty-stricken kingdom. And it has its nightingale bellowing louder than a cow, its blackbird without voice, its sheep in wolf's clothing, and its dove fiercer than any beast.

Therefore let us flee from physical, unclean love, whose sting is in its tail, however pleasing its face. Its flower is poisonous, and its bosom bears hidden serpents; its scent

3. Deuteronomy 32 : 33.

The Fire of Love

cuts the soul off from God, and its baths are warmed by the fires of hell; its gold turns to ashes, and its incense gives out sulphurous fire. Here is love without mercy, madness full of lust, which does not let the soul it has bound sit with the saints, or delight in divine love.

To those who are set on loving worldly creatures it seems burdensome and quite unbearable to think about God, although such recollection would be sweet indeed, and wonderfully delightful to them.

But if they begin to think of God, he immediately escapes their mind, and they revert to their original thoughts, on which through their own choice they have dwelt so long. They are bound, of course, by their own evil habit, and minds so weak and impure will have no taste for angels' food – at least, not without great and protracted exercise in spiritual thinking, and the rejection of physical imaginations. Their heart's palate has been defiled by their fevered, wicked love, and has made it impossible to know the sweetness of heavenly joy. Even were good thoughts to come into their minds now and then, they would not stay there. The signs of divine inspiration are at once rejected by their deep-rooted evil, so they go from bad to worse, and their ruin is all the more damnable for not accepting the good which touched them.

Thus the elect who are wholly consumed with love for God, and who cling very close to Christ, when evil or dirty thoughts sometimes knock at their souls and try to force an entry, look up at once to heaven, reject them, and quench them by their fervent earnestness. Little wonder they encourage themselves by their own good habits, so that they accept nothing earthly for themselves, or any other baneful delight which could have pleased them. For a man who is on fire with perfect charity feels neither sin nor any sort of wicked attraction; rather, he rejoices in his God, and no distress or uncleanness can upset him.

CHAPTER 39

*The manifold friendships between good men and bad;
whether they can be broken; the rarity of friendships
between men and women; true friendship, which the elect
delight in on their way; the folly of some whose abstinence
is too strict or stark; carnal friendship; male and female
fashions.*

FRIENDSHIP is a linking of wills, a mutual agreement on
this thing, a dislike of that. Friendship can exist between
good people and between bad, though the motives are
different. The greatest friendship ought to be between God
and the soul, who is expected to conform her will always to
his, so that what God wants, she wants too; what he does
not want, neither does she. In this way there will be complete friendship between them.

In human affections where there is true friendship it
would be dreadful if physical distance caused a separation
of souls; rather, an unbreakable bond of close friendship
ought to lighten the sorrow of physical absence, so that a
man feels he is still close to his friend all the while he can
see their wills constant and unbroken. For friendship is true
when one friend acts towards another as he would to himself; when his friend is his *alter ego*, loved for his own sake,
and not because he is useful, or because there is a hope of
getting something out of him.

It will be asked whether the friendship must be dissolved
if the other friend goes wrong? Some would consider it not
to be really perfect friendship unless it is one between those
who share the same values. But can it ever have been perfect if it breaks up when one party goes astray? It is certainly not perfect now, if it can gradually fade away to
nothing – which is *not* the meaning of true friendship,
which loves a man for himself, and not because he is useful
or nice. Among friends surely it is not necessary for one to
be changed just because the other is. But since it is a virtue,

it is impossible for friendship to peter out if a man has not altered in some sort. It is not necessarily broken because the other has erred: if it is a true friendship there will be all the more anxiety to reclaim the wanderer. And so that friendship by which a man seeks and secures good for his friend as if it were himself must be called *love* and while they live no misdemeanour is going to break it.

But friendship is easily broken when in the friend concerned there are not found those things for which he is loved; for instance, when there are not in the friendship things helpful or pleasant, for which sake the friends are now loved. Such friendship is spurious; it cannot last, or if it does it is only while there is pleasure and benefit in it. But what causes true friendship does not collapse while friends live. True friendship does not break down while the friends are alive, though one can go astray during that time. But even if one does err the friendship will persist if it is a true one, because they love each other as themselves, for the good that is in them. 'Good' must be understood to mean 'good by nature' rather than 'good by behaviour'.

Nature makes a man seek a loyal friend for himself, for it is natural to want to keep loyalty and gratitude. Nothing happens without reason, therefore the friendship that is natural will not dissolve while nature exists unless the natural thing loved is repugnant and harmful to nature itself. And anyway, nature cannot do that unless it has been beset by corrupt behaviour. Therefore friendship which is kindled by something different from the reason for its being loved fades and dies when the thing which excited the love cannot be had; so that if behaviour or wealth or beauty maintain the friendship, then when behaviour misbehaves, or wealth disappears, or beauty fades, friendship also vanishes, and it is said of the man who had it that 'nothing is more unhappy than to have been happy'.

But friendship that nature produces in friends is not put off by poverty, or abandoned because of error, or cancelled by deformity, all the while the nature lasts which is the cause of that friendship. Such a friendship is purely natural, and morally indifferent – unless it is scheming something against the laws of God. With it goes great enjoyment, which again is morally indifferent. For true friendship cannot exist without mutual enjoyment and pleasant fellowship and helpful conversation. And if this friendship is founded in God's grace, and is wholly his, related and directed to him, it can then be called a holy friendship, and it is very rewarding. But if through this friendship something contrary to the will of God is done by the friends, the friendship is perverted, foul and unclean, and without any merit whatever.

I cannot account for this lamentable fact but a true friend is seldom or scarcely ever found. Everybody is concerned about his own interests, and no one has a friend of whom he can say 'he is my other self'. For people pursue their own profit and pleasure, and do not blush to deceive their very friends. It is plain that they are friends not in truth but in pretence, because it is not their fellows they love so much as their goods or flatteries or favours.

But friendship between men and women can be a tricky business because a pretty face all too easily attracts a weak soul, and visual temptation kindles carnal lust, often to produce a defiled mind and body. Familiarity between women and men is apt to turn to virtue's disadvantage. And yet that sort of friendship is not improper, but rewarding, if it is practised with a good intention, and is loved for God's sake, and not for carnal delectation.

If women, say, saw that they were despised by men they would complain of God who had created them such. Perhaps they might even despair of salvation, for they feel themselves lost if they do not get advice and help from men. Reason undoubtedly is less lively in them, and so they are easily led astray and quickly overcome. They are in much need of the counsel of good men. They are attracted to evil by evil men because they are much more disposed to the pleasures of lust than to the radiance of sanctity. Yet there is a certain love that man has for woman and woman for man which none of us is without, not even the saint. It is both natural and 'instituted of God' in origin, and through it we exist, and fit in with each other, and enjoy instinctively each other's company. Indeed this delightful thing has its own pleasures, as for example in mutual conversation, or seemly contact, or a happy marriage. Yet a man does not get any merit for this unless it is filled by charity, nor does he lose any unless it is fouled by evil. But if the urge to sin rises up so that they think lustfully, and give rein to it, then they are guilty of death undoubtedly, because they are sinning against God.

So they are utterly wrong who assert that all our actions, inward or outward, are matters of reward or punishment. They are trying to deny, or at any rate are refusing to allow, that we do certain things because we like doing them, and it is natural for us to do them! They are not afraid of introducing confusion into our splendid nature.

Admittedly friendship and familiarity between men and women is wrong and forbidden if thereby they indulge the voluptuous pleasure of carnal love, and come together in their vile passion. They put eternal things behind them for passing enjoyment, and seek to excel in physical lovings. It is those who have taken Holy Orders who sin most grievously and notably. They accost these poor women like the sinners they are, and tell them they are overwhelmed with love for them, and are being gradually overcome by intense desire, and the struggle they are having with their thoughts; and so they lead these fickle and feckless creatures on to misery, in this life and the next. But they themselves will not remain unpunished, for they bear their own condemnation with them. It is of them the Psalmist speaks when he says, *their throat is an open sepulchre; with their tongues they have dealt treacherously. O God, judge them.*[1]

For God does not want women to be despised by men or to be seduced by their vain flattery, but to be instructed by them faithfully and lovingly in all that is holy and pious for the salvation of body and soul. But the man to do this is rarely found nowadays; rather (and this is the pity of it)

1. Psalms 5:9.

short

176

men are keen to teach them because it is either their belongings or their beauty they are after. So it often happens that when they instruct them in one thing, they destroy or confuse them in another, and they neither wish nor have the courage to forbid those things that women like using (even though they are sinful) so as not to offend them.

But true friendship strengthens lovers, and consoles minds, relieves grief, expels worldly depression, reforms sinners, increases holiness, decreases wrongdoing, and multiplies the rewards of the good! A man is drawn away from evil by the sound advice of his friend; he is inspired to do good when he sees in him the grace he longs to have in himself. Holy friendship is not to be despised therefore; it has the remedy for every ill. It is of God that we should be sustained amid the tribulations of our exile by the advice and assistance of friends, until we come to God himself. Then we *shall all be taught of him*,[2] blessed, and set by him in everlasting seats. We shall glory endlessly in him we have loved, through whom and for whom we have our friends.

I can except no one from friendship of this kind however holy he may be, because he needs it ... unless perhaps there is one to whom angels minister, and not men. There are some, however, who rejoice in God's love, and are so intoxicated with his sweetness that they can say, '*My soul refuses to be comforted* by earthly things'[3] (that is the comfort with which lovers of this world console themselves). But both nature and grace oblige them to take pleasure in their fellow men and in those things the body needs. Who eats or sleeps, or shelters from heat or cold, without pleasure? Or who has a friend and does not delight in his presence and conversation and company and fellowship? No one, to be sure, unless he is mad or lacking. Because it is in these things and such like that human life is comforted (even when it is most holy) and rejoices more abundantly in God. It is not of such things therefore that *My soul refuses to be comforted* is to be understood, but of the foul, un-

2. John 6:45.   3. Psalms 77:2.

clean, illicit comforts of the world. For afterwards the Psalmist said, *You have delighted me, Lord, with your doings, and in the works of your hands will I rejoice.*[4] Who can deny receiving comfort who admits to rejoicing in the works of God? *But the unwise man does not understand this and the foolish does not consider it.*[5]

Some, indeed, *have a zeal for God, but not according to knowledge,*[6] for while they are set on cutting out the frills they are also, most unwisely, induced to cut out the necessities as well, believing they cannot please God unless they afflict themselves with excessive abstinence and unrestrained destitution. And although a pale face is the proper adornment of the solitary, the service that such men render is not properly controlled, for when they are bidden to chastise their bodies, and subject them to the spirit, they are not therefore expected to kill them, but to preserve them for the honour of God until he himself who joined them separates soul from body. Such men make life difficult for their fellows, and hard for themselves, for they do not know how to retain friendship because they have never practised it.

The love of one's relatives if it is uncontrolled can indeed be called 'carnal affection', and it must be broken, because it hinders one from loving God. But if it is restrained, it can be called 'natural', for it does not affect one's service of God, and nature in this way does not act against nature's Maker.

Lastly, the women of today need to be rebuked, for to adorn their heads as well as their bodies they have invented new fashions of great and fantastic conceit, and have introduced these concoctions so as to strike spectators with horror and amazement! Not only are they going against the word of the apostle[7] with their gold, and braided hair (slaves as they are to show and licence!), but, further, against human propriety and God-ordered nature they put widespreading horns on their heads, extremely horrible, made up of hair not their own. Some of them, in their anxiety either to veil their shame or to increase their

4. Psalms 92:4.
5. Psalms 92:6.
6. Romans 10:2.
7. 1 Peter 3:3.

beauty, colour and whiten their faces with make-up, with fraudulent deceit. Men and women alike in their excessive vanity wear clothes cut in the latest style, regardless of natural decency, and only caring for what gossip and rumour and the latest fashion bring up – all at the suggestion of the devil! If anyone even occasionally wants to rebuke such things, he is laughed at; they pay greater attention to tittle-tattle than to amendment of life, so on they go and down, ensnared and seduced, those ladies (and women!) who are 'artless', and who want to be beautified in time, and de-faced in eternity. Because once the glory has faded they are going to feel the pain of hell. In this life they loved, not Christ, but the basest of worldly vanities, crowning them-selves with rosebuds before they withered![8]

But now let us go on to other things.

CHAPTER 40

At all times and in all deeds there must be room for the love of God, which does not fail in prosperity or adversity; its excellence and its comparison; tears which are turned to song.

THE love of the Godhead that gets right into a man and inflames him with the fire of the Holy Spirit, takes his soul to itself with marvellous joy; nor does it let him lose for a single moment the recollection of such love. It so controls the lover's mind that he does not bother about vanities, but is wholly directed to his Beloved.

If we are true lovers of our Lord Jesus Christ we can certainly think of him while, for example, we are travelling, and retain our song of love when we are in company: we can keep him in mind at meals even when we are enjoying food and drink. But at every bite or sip we ought to praise God, and in between the pauses when we are taking our food and scraps we ought mentally to sound his praises

8. cf. Wisdom 2:8.

with honeyed sweetness, longing and yearning for him even during meals. If we are working with our hands what is to stop our heart rising heavenward, holding tight to the thought of eternal love? At every moment we will be fervent, not sluggish, and nothing but sleep will take our heart off him.

What joy and happiness infuses the lover! What happy and desirable sweetness fills his soul! For love when it is set and made firm in Christ will always mean life without end. Neither prosperity nor adversity can alter that love, that loving desire, which is rooted in heavenly places, as those who know best have written. For, not surprisingly, it turns night to day and darkness to light, sadness to song, punishment to pleasure, and toil to sweetest rest.

For this love is not imaginary or simulated, but true and perfect, utterly set on Christ, resonant with harmonious melody to the Beloved. And if indeed you love like this, as I have shown, you too will be most glorious, keeping company with the best and most honoured in the kingdom of God, and granted the vision that gives life. And meanwhile all the assaults of the devil, and all the impulses which spring from the flesh, and all the greed for worldly things, you will valiantly overcome through the fervour of love and the power of prayer. In addition, you will conquer your pleasure in seeming beauty, for you will not want there to be even one blemish caused by your thoughts. Moreover you will abound with inner refreshment, and experience the delights of eternal love, so that you know with absolute certainty and real knowledge that you are the lover of the Eternal King. Yet none of this happens to a man unless God gives it him, or unless he is aware that even in this life no small part of his future reward is already truly dwelling in his heart.

But why do I speak of these things with others who although they are the chosen yet do not possess this choicest prize? Sometimes I wonder at myself that I have spoken of the privilege of the lovers of God as if 'whosoever will' could reach it – when it is not for him who wants it or runs after it, but for him whom Christ loves, and exalts, and receives to himself. In fact my little mind did not know how to open up what in my babbling way I was trying to make clear; yet I felt obliged to say something about the ineffable, so that those who hear or read might strive to imitate it, and find that divine love, in comparison with which all love for the most beautiful, lovable things in the world is pain and grief.

Therefore see and understand; know how very wonderful God makes his lover, how he bears him up to the heights, how he will not let him be cast down by unworthy love or vain hope, but will keep him secure in himself to be loved most sweetly. For love is a continual meditation with an immense longing for what is beautiful, good, and lovely. If anything I am loving is beautiful but not good, plainly I am not fit to love; but if it is good as well, it must be loved.

But to love a creature, however good and beautiful, is not permitted me, because I ought to offer and keep all my love for the Fount of goodness and beauty, that he may be my love who is my God and my Jesus. For he alone has in himself beauty and goodness, for he is beauty and goodness itself. Nothing else is beautiful or good unless he makes it so, and the nearer it is to him, the more beautiful and good it is. It is highly proper, then, that he should be loved who contains within himself all things that are sought by the lover. For his part he holds nothing back, so that he may be loved most fervently. But if I love something else, my conscience will prick me because I am not loving rightly. I am always afraid that what I am loving will not love me in return. And even if I am not afraid of this, I am still terrified of death which isolates those who do not love rightly from what they love, and devastates all their vanity.

Moreover, other snags often arise to disturb the serenity and enjoyment of those who love. But as for the man who loves God truly and wholeheartedly, the more fervent he knows his love for God to be, the clearer his conscience becomes. By experience he discovers that the One whom he loves is also the greatest of lovers, and death itself is not going to sever him from his sweetness. On the contrary, when he passes from this world he will find his Love to perfection, and will be united to him in truth. Thereafter he will never be separated from him; he will hasten with all speed towards that most delightful of all embraces for he will see him without veil, him whom he has loved and longed for, and will glory in him forever.

Consequently I liken this love to some inextinguishable fire, which no adverse force can quench, nor soft blandishment overcome. This love purges our sins, and its immense heat consumes all those obstacles which hinder loving; in the flaming blaze of God's love it makes us purer than gold, and brighter than the sun. This love brings us spiritual healing, and I fancy there is nothing among all the things that the learned may tell us which can so sustain and soothe us, so cleanse us from the filth of sin, as fervent love of the Godhead, and the constant recollection of our Maker.

Tears will do to wash us from our faults, and heartfelt grief will cancel our condemnation, but ardent love unimaginably surpasses all these, for it makes our soul outstandingly resplendent. More than anything else we can do, it gains the heart of the Eternal King. It deserves to contemplate him in joyous song!

I am not saying there is no point in weeping, nor am I saying that heartfelt grief is improper, or not to be desired in our exile here. Yet the man I admire is the one who has been so rapt in joy and love that he does not weep in his devotions and prayers and meditations. I would judge that to be the truer prayer and meditation when a man's love is great enough to turn his prayer into song, so that he melts into a melody of heavenly sweetness, and produces sounds angelic rather than human, anointed as he is with honeyed fervour. He is taken up, not to lament, but to shout with joy. His tears are drawn off, as it were, and he gives himself wholly over to rejoice in the Fount of true and eternal joy. The experts are forever declaring that the perfect ought to weep, and that the more perfect they are the more abundant their tears, as much for the miseries of life as for the delay in attaining our homeland. Yet to me it has meant a wonderful longing flowing out in love to God; and the sorrow of physical weeping has stopped before this vast inner sweetness. A man not consumed with eternal love must needs be purged with tears; but for him who longs with the love of eternity, love is sufficient punishment. No wound is more serious – or more sweet – than that of love. If indeed such a man would try to weep, he could not do it. This is especially true of his private devotion, for since he is being uplifted by the Holy Spirit, his mind too is being raised, and with delightful, angelic sweetness he sings his praise and his loving thoughts to God. The seat of love is high exalted, for it has extended even to the height of heaven: it seems to me to be on earth too, artfully and skilfully making men who were once lovely, wan and pale. It makes them wither, so that they may become fresh; and become weak, so as to be strong. Thus he draws close to the quiet of eternal glory and, undaunted, mingles with those who praise their Maker. The more fervently he loves the more sweetly he sings, and the more delightfully does he feel what he so strongly desired. For although to those who do not love God the way seems rough and long, it is love nevertheless which unites God and man, and with a little toil is the making of those who practise it.

CHAPTER 41

Perfect love unites a man to God inseparably, and makes him mindful of him; love of the world dissolves into nothingness; the nature of true love is steady, lasting, sweet, easy, and beneficial; false love is poisonous, disgraceful, and rotten.

WE have done the work perfectly if we have genuinely stopped our minds from loving creatures, and have joined them to God alone, in truth and completely: the more perfectly we do this, the better we are. This work is superior to every other kind, since everything we do is referred to this same end: our perfect union with God. But many things would draw us away from this; for instance, the delightful beauty of the world, male and female vanity, wealth and honours, praise and popular favour. So we have got to apply ourselves to finish the task, putting behind us and forgetting all those things that hinder.

For the love to which we are rising by this work is hotter than any burning coal, and will undoubtedly leave its mark on us, because it will make our spirits glowing and splendid. Here is love which cannot be deceived by anything created, or cheated of its eternal, heavenly reward. Yet who could long sustain the flame of this love if it were always to persist in this way? But often it is tempered lest it should consume our nature which, through the corruptible body, weighs down the soul. The corruptible flesh does not allow our mind to be lifted Godwards all the time.

The fervour of real devotion can be interrupted by sleep or by immoderate physical exercise or work; yet the ardour itself is not extinguished, even if it is not felt in the same way as previously. It returns to us when we return to God, and helps us to recover from our weakmindedness, and restores to us once more our sweetness. Furthermore, it even frees the body from all sorts of disease while keeping us sober and temperate. And it raises our souls to heavenly desires, so that we find no pleasure in the lesser things of earth.

This is the love which lays hold of Christ, and brings him into our hearts; which sweetens our minds so that in our hearts we burst out singing our hymns of praise, rejoicing in spiritual music. I believe that there is no pleasure to compare with this, which intoxicates with genuine sweetness, and delights with holy charm. The soul that receives it is purged by sacred fire, and nothing remains in it of decay or darkness. All is permeated with its lovely pleasure, so that our inner nature seems to be turned into divine glory and a song of love. Thus does the eternal love cheer us as it pours in its delightful abundance. None of its friends need yield now to creaturely or worldly affection, since they have been taken up freely into the praise and the love of Christ Jesus.

Learn then to love him who is your Cause if you want to live when you pass from here. Let your actions show that you love God now if you are wanting to live after death. Give your mind to him who is able to keep it from sorrow, here and in eternity. Never let your heart be separated from him however beset you may be by adversity and wretchedness; then you will be able joyfully to possess him, and love him for ever. You will show yourself his true lover if you never let go the remembrance of God in good times or bad.

> Good Jesus who gave me life,
>> lead me on to love you as well,
>> me, sighing for this very thing.
> Take for yourself my whole purpose,
>> so as to be my entire desire.
> Let nothing influence my heart save you!
> Sorrow and trouble would flee from me,
>> and what I covet would come
>> had only my soul heard and accepted
>> the song of your praise.
> Let your love dwell in us forever;
>> let us feel it always abiding with us.
> Therefore by your power,
>> make my thinking steadfast
>> so that it is never frittered away
>> in silly useless fantasies,
>> never laughed at for its mistakes,
>> never subject to earthly bliss or love or praise.
> But let my mind be purified by you,
>> so that it burns with love for you,
>> so that nothing can cool it,
>> be it sudden or expected.

But if I have loved anything created in this world, and it has pleased my wants in every way, and if I have sought my enjoyment in it, and made it the aim of my wellbeing and desire, then when the time comes I might well dread the burning, bitter parting. For whatever happiness I have in love of this sort, in the end there is nothing but weeping and worry, and, as it gets near, that pain which is going to punish the soul most bitterly.

Every pleasure which men in their exile think well of is like grass; now it is flourishing and green, and then it disappears as if it had never been. And undoubtedly this is how it appears to those who look at worldly joy in the right way. To those who are looking for comforts in their captivity, such joy never remains the same; it is always changing until it completely vanishes. Of course all men live in toil and trouble, and no one can avoid it. But the nature of love that is genuine and not sham is this, that it goes on, continuing steadfast, and does not change with each fresh event.

Therefore the life that can find love, and know it truly, is converted from sorrow to unspeakable joy, and lives in secret song. It will love singing, and as it rejoices in Jesus it will be like the little bird that sings till it dies. In death too it will not lack the comforting song of charity – always assuming that one does die, and not pass alive to the Beloved. And at length, when he has passed over, he will be wondrously uplifted to praise his Maker; he will overflow as he sings with indescribable joy; he will stand up amid the seraphs applauding God, that he may praise, and shine, and serve for ever and ever. And there will be love's embrace, and lovers' sweetness, and the joining of hearts, and the union of dear ones which will last through eternity. That honeyed mouth will kiss so tenderly, and the love of each for the other will know no end.

The presence of my Beloved produces immense joy and confidence, and with him I forget all my trouble. All opposition vanishes, and no other affections and lusts present themselves: silenced, they have disappeared. He alone refreshes me and hugs me to himself, he alone whom my mind has so ardently wanted. If you have loved Christ with all your will, you will loathe all squalid evil; and you will surrender your heart to him who redeemed it. Then it will be he who possesses you by his grace, and not the devil through your sin. As your soul sought Christ truly and without flinching, refusing to give up the search until she found him, so you will be led on to eternal glory and be present with your God in the seat of the blessed. So I advise you to love as I have been explaining, and take your place with the angels!

See that you do not sell this glory and honour for any vile vanity or voluptuous purpose. Take very good care that creature-love does not shut you out of the Creator's love. On earth, indeed, fear no wretchedness except that which can throw down and confound your pure love, because *perfect love is strong as death, and true jealousy is as cruel as the grave.*[1] Love is an easy burden, and not at all onerous; rather it is helpful to its bearer. It rejoices old and young alike; in it defeaters of demons delight, their prey a prisoner; by it fighters against the world and the flesh are protected. Love is a spiritual wine, intoxicating the minds of the elect, making them vigorous and manly, so that they forget the poisonous delight of the world, not bothering so much to think of it as to despise it heartily.

Therefore from holy love no lover can be the loser, but rather he stands to gain much. If he holds on to it faithfully in his heart, love without pain will dwell in the lover's soul, as indeed lovers have always proclaimed; because love makes progress, while pain destroys, and progress and destruction are complete opposites. Therefore a heart which is perfectly loving does not feel pain or worry, nor is it sad or troubled: perfect love and grievous misery are incompatible. Again, what is done gladly is not done sadly. A lover indeed works freely and gladly, and so work to him is happy, not irksome; he is under no obligation and he has no complaints, so he always shows himself cheerful and gay.

Love therefore is the sweetest and most useful thing a rational creature can ever acquire. Most acceptable and pleasing to God, it not only binds the soul with bands of

1. Canticles 8:6.

wisdom and sweetness when it joins it to God, but it also restrains flesh and blood, so that a man does not go after mistaken delights, or wander off in search of error of various kinds. Through love of this kind the heart grows healthy, and our life finds meaning and strength. Little wonder then that I have never found a better dwelling-place – or sweeter. For love unites my love and me, and makes of two one.

Yet carnal love will flourish and perish like some wild flower of summer, for its joy and existence will seem no more than a single day's duration, so sure is it to last but a short while and then decline in sorrow. This also will undoubtedly be the bitter lot of those who love vanity. Their pride, their toying with unreal beauty, will be flung out into the filth and shame which is to be theirs when they are cast into endless torment. And this will never pass away, unlike their specious happiness and their joy in shining beauty which have now passed into nothingness: all those things in which they once delighted have gone for ever.

But God does give men and women beauty, not of course that they should burn in love for each other and despise their Maker – as nowadays nearly everybody does – but that they should recognize it as a favour of the Lord their God, and glorify him with their whole heart, and love him without ceasing; so that they should constantly yearn for that unfading beauty compared with which all worldly beauty and glory is nothing. For if loveliness of the form is to be seen among the servants of the world, what will be the beauty of the sons of God set in heaven? Therefore let us love him fervently, because if we have loved we shall sing to Christ with sweet-voiced and delightful melody. His love conquers all things. Therefore let us live in love, and in it die!

CHAPTER 42

The sweetness and happiness of the love of God; the song of the nightingale; a prayer for the continuation of genuine, spiritual song, not had by lovers of the world.

I know no pleasure sweeter
than in my heart to sing you a song of praise, Jesus my
   love.
I know no happiness greater or more abundant
than in my mind to feel the sweet warmth of love.

I believe that the very best thing one can ever do is to fix Jesus in one's heart, and never want anything else. He has made a good start in loving who has loving tears, and a sweet yearning and desire for eternal things. For Christ himself yearns, so to speak, for our love, when he hastened with such fervour to his Cross to redeem us. But it is truly said that 'love precedes the dance, and gives the lead'. It was nothing but love which brought Christ so low.

Come, my Saviour, comfort my soul!
Make me steadfast in my love for you,
so that I never cease loving.
Take the grief from me when it is my time to die,
   for there is no sinner who cannot rejoice
   once he be perfectly converted to you.
Remember your compassion, Jesus most sweet,
   that my life may shine resplendent in your power;
   and so that I can overcome my enemy
   bestow on me your mighty salvation!
I ask all this of you lest I be lost with the son of perdition.
Since my mind has been fired with holy love,
   I am filled with longing to see your Majesty.
Therefore I endure poverty,
   I despise earthly dignity,
   and I care for no sort of honour.

Your friendship is my glory.
When I began to love, your love laid hold of my heart,
   and would allow me to desire nothing save love.
Then you, God, made my soul flame with your sweet
      light,
   so that in you and through you
   I could die and not feel sad.
There is delightful warmth in the loving heart,
   which has consumed gloom and trouble in its fiery
      burning love.
And from it has issued sweetness,
   and in particular, music which comes in to soothe the
      soul,
   for there you, my God and my comfort,
   have set up your Temple.

Very delightful indeed is the glory I yearn for, and no
man can be more earnest in such longing than I. Therefore
my loving soul, adorning herself as a bride for the King
Emperor, says, 'Love lays hold of my heart with unspeakable bands, and enslaves and entwines it with such vigour
and wonderful mastery, that it likes to think it would rather
die than live.' This flower cannot perish; so ardent is my
Friend in love that he fuses together joy and death and
song!

When first I was converted, and became single-minded, I
used to think I would be like the little bird which pines for
love of its beloved, but which can rejoice in the midst of its
longing when he, the loved one, comes. While it sings its
joy, it is still yearning, though in sweetness and warmth. It
is said that the nightingale will sing her melody all night
long to please him to whom she is united. How much more
ought I to sing, and as sweetly as I can, to my Jesus Christ,
my soul's spouse, through the whole of this present life.
Compared with the coming brightness this life is 'night',
and I too languish, and languishing, faint for love. But because I faint I shall recover, and be nourished by his
warmth; and I shall rejoice, and in my joy sing jubilantly

the delights of love. Flute-like, I shall pour out melodious,
fervent devotion, raising from the heart songs of praise to
God Most High. Already they have been offered by mouth,
an earnest of the praise of God, because my soul is ever avid
to love; never through grief or sloth will she give up her
accepted desire.

Indeed, integrity of purpose, readiness of will, fervour of
real desire, and conversion to God, if they are continually
thought of – as they are by holy souls – do not allow them
to sin mortally. And should they have sinned through
weakness or ignorance, at once they are stirred to true penitence by these same stimuli, so they do not dwell long in
sin, even if they have clung to its enjoyment. The venial
sins they commit are wholly burnt up in the fire of love,
unless perhaps some have been so affected by negligence
that they no longer consider it a sin in which they offend
and they have not enough charity to wipe out all the punishment due to them, or there is no tribulation by which
their fault can be purged. But in the coming of love the
heart of the lover blazes up. Hotter than fire is this wonderful heat, which rejoices the mind so sweetly, and gives
coolness and shade from the heat of sins.

> Good Jesus, bestow on me the rich melody
>   and heavenly song of the angels,
>   so that, enraptured, I may ever chant your praises.
> What you gave me once when I neither knew nor
>   understood
>   give me again now that I am experienced and am ask-
>   ing for it!
> Fondle me with joyful, heavenly love,
>   so that at my last hour I am found crowned with fire!
> With a song of joy come into my soul.
> Show me something of your sweetness and charm when
>   you so please,
>   so that here my transgressions may be punished and
>   purged,
>   because in your mercy you have known him

as one who clings closely to you.
But do not show me how you deal in your wrath
  with those who flourish in the world,
  on whom you lavish temporal blessings,
  and for whom you reserve everlasting torment!
Those who love the world can indeed know
  the words or verses of our songs, but not their music;
  for though they read the words they cannot add the
    note or the tone
  to the sweetness of our love-songs.

Good Jesus, you have bound my heart
  to think of your Name, and now I cannot but sing it.
So pity me by perfecting what you have planned.
Your true, solicitous lover, thinking of these things,
  is so rapt into joyful praise that it is quite impossible
  for such sweetness to come from the devil,
  such fervour to be of any created thing,
  such music to spring from human wit.
If I have persevered in these things I shall be saved.

It is only right that he who wishes perfectly to avoid
great sins should not willingly commit even the smallest
ones. For he who knowingly and freely falls in small ways,
often carelessly runs headlong into greater. It is the nature
of love that it would wish rather to incur the greatest
misery than to sin but once. No need compels a man to seek
pleasure and wealth, strength and beauty here; on the
contrary, it would be the height of absurdity for one who
in the purpose of the Eternal King is intended to be made a
knight, seemly in limb, fair and splendid, rightly propor-
tioned. And there in the court of heaven he will serve the
Emperor Most High for ever and ever.